Praise for Sun Tzu Was a Sissy

"A hilarious, thought-provoking war plan for the battlefield of the modern workplace. Bing proves once and for all that the pen is mightier than the sword, especially when he's wielding the pen and the guy with the sword has been dead for thousands of years."
   —Neil Cavuto, Fox News

"Bing is hilarious!"
   —Don Imus

"This sarcastic, sardonic little work is a real gem."
   —Liz Smith

"Among our best corporate-war correspondents. Bing provides a wickedly entertaining little guide to remaking yourself as a rapacious, coldhearted S.O.B."
   —*Time*

"Mr. Bing's humor is...laugh-out-loud funny."
   —*Dallas Morning News*

"A masterful curmudgeon who causes laugh-out-loud moments."
   —*USA Today*

About Stanley Bing

Stanley Bing is a columnist for *Fortune* magazine and the best-selling author of *What Would Machiavelli Do* and *Throwing The Elephant*, as well as the novel *You Look Nice Today* and the ultimate guide to life in this or any other workplace world, *The Big Bing*. By day, he is an haute executive in a gigantic multinational corporation whose identity is one of the worst-kept secrets in business. His stomping ground is New York City.

Sun Tzu Was a Sissy

Conquer Your Enemies, Promote Your Friends, and Wage

The *Real* Art of War

STANLEY BING

An Imprint of HarperCollinsPublishers

HarperCollins books may be purchased for educational, business, or sales pro-
motional use. For information, please write: Special Markets Department,
HarperCollins Publishers, 10 East 53rd Street, New York, NY 10022.

First Collins paperback edition 2006.

Library of Congress Cataloging-in-Publication Data is available upon request.

ISBN-13: 978-0-06-073478-7
ISBN-10: 0-06-073478-7

06   07   08   09   10   ❖/RRD   10   9   8   7   6   5   4   3   2   1

to Alexander the Great,
who wept when there were no more worlds to conquer . . .

to Bobby Fischer,
who never got the message that chess is just a game,
and made his opponents cry . . .

to Bill Gates,
for sometimes not having the good taste to play fair . . .

to George W. Bush,
for his determination to finish up his father's war
no matter what . . .

and to the guys who run the corporation for which I work,
who are always angry about something.

The art of war is of vital importance to the state. It is a matter of life or death, a road either to safety or to ruin. One ignores it at one's peril.

Sun Tzu

Of course you know ... this means war!

Bugs Bunny,

to Elmer Fudd

Contents

Acknowledgments

I'd like to thank a bunch of people for generating in me the hostility that made this book possible.

I'd like to thank Mr. Danacus, my gym teacher in fourth grade, for calling me "fatso" in front of Barbara Michaels while I was roller skating at the Police Athletic League one Friday evening a long, long time ago. If I saw him dead on the street right now, I would kick his lifeless body.

I'd like to thank Jerry Wise for making fun of my blue jeans back in sixth grade. How was I supposed to know that everybody had switched over to chinos?

I'd like to thank Alan Albert, my first boss, for exploiting a bunch of impoverished actors to the tune of $85 per week while he was pocketing big fees for the "educational workshops" the federal government thought we were teaching.

I'd like to thank my first chairman, Dan, for promoting Linda, a weeping crybaby moldering behind her office door, over me, the guy who really ran the department—an act that filled me with so much pure, white-hot hatred and cynicism that I still have fantasies of poking him in the eyes with two fingers, the way Moe used to do to Curly.

To the head of my now-dead corporation, Doug, who divested us to bump up the value of his stock options, throwing all my friends out of work and crippling our company so that it never quite recovered. What a bozo. Hi, Doug!

In fact, to all the Nords whose stupidity, cupidity, and arrogance have deluded them into thinking that it pays in any way to oppose me.

They'll get theirs.

Preface

Sun Tzu,
a Sissy for Our Times

> Therefore, one hundred victories in one hundred battles
> is not the most skillful. Subduing the other's military
> without battle is the most skillful.
> **Sun Tzu**

> War is not nice.
> **Barbara Bush**

Several thousand years ago in China, or what was then destined to be China, there lived a guy named Sun Tzu. Like Nicolo Machiavelli and Walt Rostow and Paul Wolfowitz, he didn't run the world, he just advised those who did. Presumably, those he advised did better than those he didn't, even though because they're dead now that's hard to ascertain.

And so his legend grew from one generation of murderous warlords to the next, until he became more famous than they did, possibly because his name was easier to remember, but also because in general writers have the last word.

Sun Tzu wrote about War. How to make it. How to win it. How to get others to die in it instead of you. This last was particularly popular with warlords back then, and remains so to this day with their contemporary counterparts in both the military and the executive suites.

Sun Tzu wrote a bunch of extremely poetic and deep stuff that somebody must have understood, because it was handed lovingly down over the years to those who kill people for a living, and is now taught at West Point and sold, in one form or another, in airport bookstores to people in charge of marketing and advertising and even Human Resources.

Why Sun Tzu is appealing to people is a mystery, because his stuff is about as easy to understand as one of those instruction manuals they give you when you buy any product from eastern Europe. Let me give you an example:

> When the enemy is near and still, he is relying on the steep. When the enemy is far and provokes battle, he wishes the other to advance—he is occupying the level and advantageous.

There's a lot of stuff like this throughout the book that's come to be known as *The Art of War*, but it all adds up to the fact that whatever Emperor Sun Tzu must have worked for, it's quite likely he had no clothes. But then, that's true of a lot of emperors. And no matter how shockingly naked the local warlord is, he probably still needs to defend himself.

It isn't that Sun Tzu was wrong, exactly. But there's no business like Tzu business, not today. His approach might have been darned good when the job was to tramp a bunch of guys in bamboo ponchos up and down the mountainside, waiting for the optimal time to swoop down and acquire the most advantageous position for the next round of fighting. I don't know about you, but I haven't come up against that situation since the late 1990s.

I fight in the real world as, I'm sure, do you. We don't really have armies, per se. Like, we have people we fight with, but armies? Sadly, no. We don't have terrain as such, either, unless you define terrain quite differently. We can do that, but Sun Tzu didn't, not really. Because he was a sissy.

I know that perhaps sounds a bit harsh. I don't mean it to be. It's quite possible that all of the Tztuff he talks about, the mincing dependence on hyperstrategy and deep philosophical musings, the delicate calibration of where, when, and how to strike, the weeny-hierarchical hagiographic view of ultrasenior management—used to work.

But we don't really live in a world where the following statement is of any particular use:

> The shuai-jan is a snake of the Chung mountains.
> Strike at its head and you will be attacked by its tail.
> Strike its tail and you will be attacked by its head.
> Strike its midsection and you will be attacked by head and tail both.

Know what? That's just too inscrutable for me. When I'm thinking about War, I don't want to prance around the maypole. I want to be rolling up my sleeves and wrapping my tie around my head. I know my adversary is probably doing the same. If he's not, he should be. Because I'm coming.

To be Tzure, the Master did have many important things to say about War that we can listen to and take into account. It's better not to fight, for instance, unless you absolutely know for sure that you're going to win. That's one of his big points. Who could deny that? Except the thing is, a lot of the time when I have to fight, I don't know if I'm going to win. I mean . . . there's that.

Then there's the whole idea that the real military genius is the one who can win without firing a shot. Like, the general is so strategic that the other guy just falls down from sheer lack of strategic advantage. I've never actually seen that happen, but there's no question at all that if you're going to have any chance at winning, you've got to have a very nice strategy going forward. It's the overreliance on strategy, however, that makes Sun Tzu such a limp biscuit at this particular point in the history of the world. Our world, at any rate. I'm sure that back when there were only half a billion Chinese he was known far and wide as a fearsome enemy and terrifying opponent. But now? No.

We can do better. We need to.

Finally, Sun Tzu talks a lot about Tao and other spiritual kinds of material like that, which, frankly, I find kind of offensive in a discussion about war, and killing, and fighting. As far as I'm concerned, let's have the good taste to leave Tao out of it, huh? Blood? Guts? Raw, animal hatred? Sure. But Tao? Come on.

Anyone who has ever seen a guy lose twenty years of expense account plastic in one afternoon will tell you there's nothing even slightly Tao about the whole business. When the check comes, he has to go to the Men's Room to avoid the possibility of kicking in his share. That's defeat by any standard.

Bottom line? The real Art of War does not come from the East anymore anyhow. Not anymore. It comes from the greatest nation in the world, the last superpower on the planet.

War is violent, scary, and the quickest way to gain and keep territory and, hopefully, your life, over time. Those wise and sage and full of Sun Tzu enough not to fight are generally fetching beverages for those who are willing to poke out somebody else's eye if need be. And Tao schmow. Wars are about hate. You don't go to war unless you want to kill the other guy.

This is neither the way things should be nor the way we wish them to be. It is simply what is. Those who want to prevail in these perilous times had better know how to wage war to win, getting deep down into the field of battle with the stink of sweat and Diet Coke in your nostrils and the tears of big, bald men all over your shoes.

This book will attempt to transcend all that Eastern goo and teach you, feisty westerner, how to make war and enjoy the subsequent booty. All of this will have to take place in the real world, which is to say not on the military playing field, or on the gridiron, or the links. The battle we wage takes place in the toughest trench of all: where we work.

It's a world where those who do not kick, gouge, and grab—and do so with a bit of style and panache, I might add—are left behind at the table to pay the tab while the winners go out to the next cool club.

We will examine it all—how to plan and execute battles that hurt other people (and not yourself) a lot, advance your flag and those of your friends, if indeed you have any. If you're going to wage war, you'd better have a whole bunch of them. You're going to need them.

And when it comes to all that sissy strategizing, don't get me wrong. Strategy is the bomb, as far as it goes. Each and all will be considered here, from mustering, equipping, organizing, plotting, and scheming to rampaging, squashing, and reaping spoils.

The reaping part, of course, is important. War without a booty call is hardly worth waging. But there is a land of violence and glory far beyond the dry strategic humping up hill and dale that characterized the old art of war. There's playing with emotion. Fighting when the end is not in sight. Living the life of the warrior, which could end at any time, and having fun while you're doing it.

The Tzumeister, for his part, was not totally useless. Perhaps, as we go, we can glean some wisdom from the elderly dude if we take him firmly by the scrotum, turn him upside down, shake him roundly, and see what pops out of his sissy silk pajamas.

Introduction

All You Need Is War

Only one thoroughly acquainted with the evils of war
can successfully wage one.
Sun Tzu

Worse than that, the pay is bad.
Burt Reynolds

What is war? The question is not as simple as it looks.

When your boss yells at you because he's in a swivet about something vaporous, is that war? Are you at war simply because you've been yelled at?

Nah. If you were at war every time some butthead yelled at you, you'd be dead by now. Of stupidity.

When you and a peer argue about the best way to do something, are you at war with that person simply because he or she disagrees with you, even in public?

Maybe, if you're at GE. But as a rule, that would be unfortunate. Disagreements happen, even between friends, and life would scarcely be worth living if every little face-off was just a skirmish in a larger battle that was part of a career-long war.

There are those who treat every human interaction as a military engagement that could escalate into a potential battle leading to a nice, satisfying conflict that's part of a war. There is a name for such people. They're called assholes.

Is it war when that same peer goes behind your back and secures the agreement of the executive you both serve, making you look like a lump of spoiled meat in the process?

Now we're getting closer.

And when the Boss is so pleased he takes that other guy out to lunch and allows him to pick up the check? And you're not invited?

Yes. That's war, all right. The pig must die. Not the senior pig, though. That senior pig is your commander under whom you serve in love and squalor alike. But the junior pig, yes, that porker must be bound, trussed, and broiled, served up in public with an apple in his or her mouth.

But how? How shall we make the art of war in the real world where we must live every day because there are pretty much no alternatives?

Shall we quietly study ourselves and search deep within our souls, wherever they may be, for our capabilities and frailties? Yeah, okay. We can do that.

Assess the terrain for possible positions of advantage and disadvantage, modulating our response accordingly? Sure. Why not?

Muster our troops? Train them? Educate them? Fill them with song and dance? Equip them with the proper tools of warfare? Map out lines of attack? Indubitably.

In the meantime, while all that good stuff is going on, why don't we just stride like Vikings up to the offending twerp and strike off his head with a large club that has several sharp spikes in its business end? Icelandic sagas are full of that kind of thing. Guys smiting heads and then watching them roll like candlepin bowling balls into a lake. It's very satisfying.

Of course, you can't go around clubbing people's heads into the lake every day for every minor infraction, no matter what a nice plopping sound they make when they hit the water. You need a range of options and approaches. Because wars come in a variety of flavors, and you can't chew just one.

Here are just a few types of wars you may encounter in a business career:

* **Itty-bitty War:** You and another guy go head-to-head. You want to win. You are General, Army, Navy, Marines, and counterintelligence. It's you and him. Only one of you will live.

* **Medium-sized War:** Your department is being attacked by a consultant from someplace that seeds Harvard MBAs into an organization the way ants lay eggs in the beams of an old house. The consultant is supported by senior management and Wall Street, which loves any kind of middle-management destruction. Your enemies are many. Your resources are few. Your only strength is the fact that you know more about your jobs than any consultant does.

* **Total Conflagration:** Donald Trump wants the ground your business is sitting on. Microsoft likes the business you're in and wants to suck it all up for itself. *The Wall Street Journal* has decided you're a poster child for Sarbanes-Oxley scrutiny. It doesn't matter. The entire state is under assault. You will, as Ben Franklin observed at the signing of the Declaration of Independence, all hang together or you will most certainly all hang separately.

* **Guerrilla War:** Snipers to the left of you. Spies to the right. It's hard to tell friend from foe. The killing has gone on for years, so long in fact that it's hard to remember why the guys in Sales want to kill everybody in Marketing. Not

enough people are destroyed on a day-to-day basis to warrant a white flag or a treaty on either side, but peace just never seems to come.

* Siege: You and your guys need more money to get the job done. Finance wants a total freeze on internal spending. Nobody says no. Nobody says yes. Time goes by. Your hands are freezing in the frigid air. Your guys are dying of exposure. Something's gotta give . . . and soon.

* The Big One: Your CEO has decided that the only way to get the stock up is to merge with your nearest competitor. It's war so vast and terrible that all human life may be expunged. They've got nukes. You've got dirty bombs in the form of close relationships with trade media reporters. The armies line up on the field of battle. In a moment, there will be the stink of cigar smoke and the clink of $600 fountain pens hitting paper. There is no future, no past, no tomorrow. There is only blood, sputum, and sorrow.

Dramatic? Sure. Ubiquitous? No doubt about it. These days war is as inescapable as the $30 omelet.

And you? You report to some kind of general. How he functions will determine a lot. And that's a problem, if you, like Tzu, are a sissy. Because one of the things about generals is that there aren't many that are any good. They want you to die well . . . and well before they do. They're under a lot of pressure. A lot of the time, too much. Can you trust your lives and futures to these guys?

Consider this, from the commander of the United States military today:

Reports that say that something hasn't happened are always interesting to me, because as we know, there are known knowns, there are things we know we know. We also know there are known unknowns. That is to say we know there are some things we do not know. But there are also unknown unknowns: the ones we don't know we don't know.

Secretary of Defense
Donald Rumsfeld

Right. You know what? I think that for our purposes, it's far better to assume that we are going to avoid placing ourselves into anybody else's hands, no matter how capable, staunch, or well connected they might be. Because, like as not, they're in it for themselves. And you? You're in it for you. This is a basic contradiction that is tolerable in peacetime. But when the bullets and bullshit are flying, it could be lethal.

So you and I, my friends, we will be our own generals in the campaign for wealth, health, and sanity, fighting our own battles, not somebody else's.

The Real Art of War

Part One

Preparing Your Bad Self

The general is the state's guardian. If he is strong, the
state is safe. If he is not, the state will crumble.
Sun Tzu

What you lookin' at, Willis?
Gary Coleman

Beyond Yin and Yang:
The Secret of Yinyang

Fate is both yin and yang. It is ice. It is fire. It is winter
and spring, summer and fall, and then winter again.
Go with it. Go against it. That is victory.
Sun Tzu

You can't win if you don't play.
Poker aphorism

War is hell. War is glory. You've got to have the ability to
sustain small losses between major victories. But like it?
No. Take it in stride? Only if you're a loser.

In battle, attitude is all. And true warriors are united in the
fact that they hate to lose even more than they love to win.
They're nuts about it. Sometimes that hatred of being on the
wrong end of the beefstick makes them do nutty things, of
course. It pays to think about that for a moment, before we go on.

I don't like to pick on Martha Stewart, because I believe she is,
in the end, a teeny newt who has been treated shockingly in comparison to the enormous, gray toads whose crimes far, far out-
strip hers and who are now all writing books somewhere waiting
for *Forbes* to do a positive retrospective on them.

But Martha had a chance, at the very beginning of her ordeal,
to admit that she kind of screwed up, acted rather badly for
someone who is both a genius and a former stockbroker, take

whatever tepid punishment the pleased, appeased, and publicity-hungry Feds were of a mind to dole out, and then, sadder but richer, soldier on.

Instead, because she couldn't bear to lose to the press, the Justice Department, or anyone else, she brought herself a world of grief and, even worse, lost a lot of money pursuing her dream of perfection.

That's too much Yang.

On the other side, there's Jerry Levin of Time Warner, perhaps pound for pound the biggest Tzu-head of the last few decades. So strategic was this teeny warrior that he strategized his entire company out of, like, 60 percent of its value in the merger with AOL. Come on, he told the ragtag bunch of scrabbly Internet dudes who couldn't find a corporate infrastructure with both hands, take us. We're yours. He assumed the position. And it took his proud empire years to undo the damage wrought by his intelligence, foresight, and pure, unadulterated Yin.

Yang never drops its sword until death has made its decision who to take.

Yin hopes that the other guy will die of a heart attack while he's stabbing you.

As you prepare yourself for the eternal struggle that is the life of the warrior, you must cultivate both not consecutively, but in unison. You must reach for both inside yourself and merge the two into the warrior attitude of both strength and flexibility, aggression and strategy, anger and the ability to swallow that anger and make a deal that will enable you to fight another day. Too much Yang makes you stupid. Too much Yin makes you a wuss.

What you need is the combo of both. You need Yinyang.

Yinyang is the point where the irrational will to power merges sinuously with the willingness to be reasonable. This mix manifests itself in a variety of ways, and is the determinant of success in war.

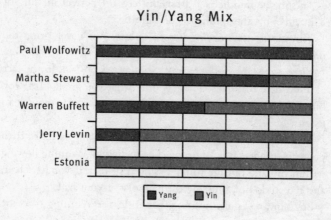

Yin/Yang Mix

Paul Wolfowitz

Martha Stewart

Warren Buffett

Jerry Levin

Estonia

Yang Yin

Too much Yang gives you war in Iraq. You get an idea in your head and nobody can turn you off it. It happens to executives all the time. You may work for one of them. If you do, you know what I'm talking about. The kind of guys who said the car would never replace the horse, that cable was a flash in the pan, that it was a good idea to build a nuclear power plant over the largest fault line in the United States or at the east end of Long Island, where it takes two hours to go down the road and buy a blueberry pie on the weekends—a fact that might have some bearing on evacuation plans? No way. Too much Yang.

Next down the chart are the executives who have just a little too much testosterone for their own good. You can be one of those. It means you will win for a while, and then lose playing the game that got you there.

At the other end of the scale, right after Time Warner, is Estonia, which has been taken over by every invading army since the invention of beer.

And in the middle is Warren Buffett, the perfect mixture of Yin and Yang, the apotheosis of Yinyang.

Yinyang is never saying Yes to failure. But never being too proud to listen to reason.

Yinyang means in the face of Yes there is no No. In the face of No, there is no Yes. There is only what you are fighting for. But if Maybe appears . . . not being too big a stiffy about it to listen.

Yinyang is power. Yinyang is money. Yinyang is more than power or money. It is Winning. The feeling of Winning flowing within you and outside you, mussing your hair, if you have hair, and if you do not, mussing the memory of your hair.

But Yinyang is also waiting, patiently, for Winning to come along.

It is Oneness, Sureness, Obnoxiousness. It is your warrior attitude. Beyond Yin. Beyond Yang. That's so Old School.

It's Yinyang.

Get some.

Are You Worth Dying For?
(I'm Guessing No)

The general is trustworthy,
brave, strict and wise.
Sun Tzu

Military Intelligence is a contradiction in terms.
Groucho Marx

Over at Enron, there was an interesting pecking order, as is now evident from the sequence in which the various well-dressed peckers are being investigated, indicted, and, covered with shame and regret (at being caught), sent to prison, where they can rat out their former friends and associates. Each one goes down, falling first on the grenade that should be taking out the big doofus who ran the place.

People say Ken Lay was an idiot who didn't know what was going on, a glad-handing fool who fiddled with his own portfolio while Rome was still promising a fabulous return on investment.

Yes, it may be "true" that he didn't "know" what was "going on" day to day with his company's "accounting practices." And yes, he was a liar and a crook and the kind of person who makes you wonder sometimes whether there really is a guiding hand that shapes our universe and, if there is, what It could possibly be thinking about.

But as a general, Ken Lay was everything Sun Tzu would want. Look at how many were willing to die for him! And not even like him very much!

What are the qualities in a leader that will make people want to perish in His or Her stead?

It's an important question, because if you're going to be a success in this war thing, you're going to need to enlist a lot of support. In the beginning, you will be alone. Your job in the early stages is to figure out how you can attract other people willing to sacrifice themselves so that you don't have to.

Before this, I'm guessing you were part of somebody else's army. That's all well and good. Somebody has to pay your lunch tab. But as of right now, everything is different.

Henceforth, my friend, you're not part of anybody else's army, you're part of your army. You ARE your army. So you won't be dying for anybody else, no matter how big and seductive they might be. There. Isn't that a relief?

Sun Tzu says:

> Tao is what causes the people to have the same purpose
> as their superior. Thus they can die with him, live with
> him and not deceive him.

The same purpose as their superior. Right . . .

Hm. Let's think about that for a minute.

When I was a young man I worked for a very good company that was very well run by very nice people who knew what they were doing. There was a lot of affection and we made everybody a lot of money. We would have walked into fire for Harold, our Chairman, and Carl, our President. Then they sold our division, and all that firewalking really did take place. The ultrasenior managers did fine, because they had one purpose—to get out of it with a conestoga of cash. The middle management did a lot less fine, because their purpose was different. Their purpose was to die protecting the executive wagon train on its way out of town.

We all recognize that kind of story, and know it's right around the bend for every one of us. And yet, we all line up every day prepared to lay down our lives for our leaders. Why? Why, when we know that, in the end, it is likely to end in tears—for us, not for them.

For fear? Possibly. But that's not enough. For greed? Yes. But not die, actually. Very few are willing to die for Greed. What else is there!

Love, of course.

Getting People to Love You
Part 1: Loving Yourself

> What counts is not necessarily the size of the dog in the
> fight—but the size of the fight in the dog.
> **Dwight D. Eisenhower**

This may sound insane to you, but just take a moment to think about it a bit: Before you can get others to die for you, you have to be willing to die for yourself. For the greater *idea* of yourself. When Mark Antony went gaga for Cleopatra, he knew he was bringing the might of Rome down upon him. He didn't care. He knew that the man called Mark Antony couldn't just go back and march around the Forum in a miniskirt anymore. He had other things to do. So he died for himself, for his idea of himself.

More recently, Howard Dean, the former governor of the tiny state of Vermont, seized the national imagination by providing an alternative to the same old stale politics that has put younger Americans, and many older ones, to sleep for the past few decades. He saw himself as a man of truth and, most critically, passion. Howard Dean's idea of Howard Dean was that Howard Dean was a man who brought passion to politics.

So when he lost Iowa in unexpected fashion, he wanted to show his followers that he still had that passion. Conceding defeat, and his intention to soldier on, he issued what has now become known as the "I Have a Scream" speech, an utterance so comically over the top that it expunged him from the race. Nobody wants to see a potential Chief Executive howling like a beagle. But in killing his own candidacy, Dean was true to the man who had the vision to become a contender in the first place. He died for himself. And that scream notwithstanding, he walked away with the respect and affection of many who value politics as something true and important and not smarmy, sticky, and repulsive.

Are you willing to die for yourself? If you want to be, you have to be able to take the very first step toward attaining that capability. You have to be willing to live for yourself.

This is a bigger commitment than it seems, but it's at the heart of all who command the kind of devotion that you're looking for from others. And it's hard. Most people want to live for others at least a little bit. You can't do that if you want to be a true business warrior.

Living for Yourself:
Key Commitments

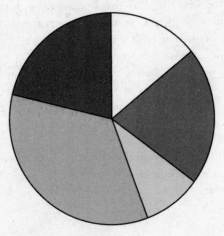

☐ Eating Well
■ Drinking the Good Stuff
☐ Being Angry All the Time
☐ Obsession with Getting Your Own Way
■ Using Other People as Tools

When you can generate a demented level of self-regard to the exclusion of all things, and do so without waking up in the middle of the night in a cold sweat, you will be ready to start demanding suicidal love from others in a business environment.

There already? Good.

Getting People to Love You
Part 2: Hello Mother, Hello Father

Give attaboys and ass-kicking in equal proportions.
Anything not built on balance will
eventually fall over.
Sun Tzu

You never call. You never write.
Your mother

Did you ever think of how many ways a boss is like a crippled, dwarfed, mutated replica of one's original authority figure—the Parent? Let us count the ways:

* Providing bread, via paychecks and periodic improvements to one's life and style;

* Demanding work of some sort on a relatively consistent basis, many times when you'd rather be doing something else;

* Requiring love or, in the case of some, an alternating current of both love and hatred;

* The tendency to be attentive at times and distracted at others;

* Never wrong, even when obviously so;

* Capable of making you feel guilty when you have done nothing wrong;

* Proudly inconsistent in pursuit of objectives that are at best unclear and at worst inexplicable;

* Slow to anger, quick to forgive . . .

No, wait a minute. That's God. We're not that far gone yet. Except at Wal-Mart, where God in the form of Sam Walton may be dead but is still carrying on much as before. Or North Korea, where God has really funny hair.

Sun Tzu taught that a rational, strategic approach to the management of people works best. Maybe he was right in some far-flung corner of the world where for a good fifty years during the twentieth century most people went around in identical pajamas. But here in the western portion of Pangaea, order and rationality give way to love and hate, passion and greed, ambition, manipulation, guilt, shame, and the occasional stab of joy. In short, family.

Psychiatrists call it *transference*. It's the process by which emotions and desires originally associated with one person, like a father or mother, brother or sister, are unconsciously shifted to another person, usually an authority figure of some kind.

Think of how you feel about the people you work for. Love them? Hate them? Resent them? Want to get things from them? Do you become irrationally giddy when they praise you for something mundane? Does a storm cloud descend on your face when they fail to greet you in the elevator? Are you jealous of the guy down the hall who just got a new name plate for his desk?

You're transferring your deepest personal emotions into your job. And it's not only natural, it's inevitable.

Now just get people to do it for you by taking the following steps immediately:

1. Be kind when you can.

2. Be angry when you can. People expect their parents to get mad at them.

3. Demand a lot of work. People expect their parents to give them chores.

4. Praise inconsistently, so that your praise means something. If you praise people too much, they think you're sucking up to them, and only rotten parents suck up to their kids.

5. Punish people with parental punishments, not business ones, like yell at them and kick them out of your office when they displease you, following that with a hurt silence for a couple of days. By the end of that kind of thing, they'll be begging to die for you.

And like all authority figures worthy of respect, obedience, and death, listen to other people occasionally, but not too much. Whose parents really listen to them?

If you follow these precepts, even those who are not required to honor and obey you will begin feeling the requirement to do so. As your mother always said, "If you don't ask, you don't get." So demand all the things that are due an irrational parent and, quite inexplicably, you will start developing a cadre of needy people who look to you for guidance, approval, and, most important, orders.

That's one step away from your first order of business: creating an army.

Keep on Truculent

Fuck you, asshole.
Arnold Schwarzenegger

Arnold Schwarzenegger is The Governor of California. Even if you live in California and voted for Arnold, doesn't that kind of whip your head around a couple of times?

Arnold Schwarzenegger is the governor of California. In a way, that's a bigger cosmological leap than Jesse Ventura being governor of Minnesota, although I guess that was pretty mind-boggling at the time as well. Jesse was in a lot of Arnold's movies, and died quite movingly in *Predator,* where he got an alien rocket through the midsection. Soon after that, he ran for governor. Think that gave Arnold some food for thought?

Now, don't tell me Arnold was elected because he has a visionary road map for the Golden State. I mean, perhaps he does, but that's not why he's in there.

No, Arnold Schwarzenegger is the governor of California because he has convinced the citizens of California that he is sufficiently truculent to do anything he wants to do. We're not talking about the nice, surprisingly intelligent and witty Austrian hedonist who says things like, "I think gay marriage is something that should be between a man and a woman," and "Money doesn't buy happiness. Now that I have fifty million I'm no happier than when I had forty-eight million."

No, we're talking about the other Arnold. The one who took

out his own eye, washed it off, and put it back in in the first *Terminator.* The one who killed, like, 10,000 guys in *Commando* because they kidnapped his daughter . . . who, in *T2,* thrust his big, muscular thumb to the sky in a supreme gesture of defiance and hope while being boiled alive in hot metal. That Arnold. The one who promises: "I'll be back." And you know he will be, too, because he's too damn mean not to.

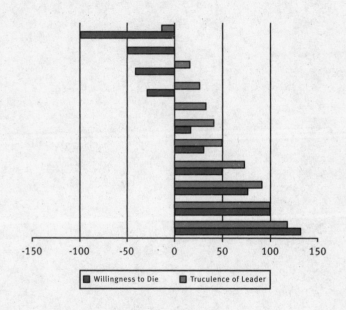

The chart on the previous page elucidates the relationship between people's Willingness to go to battle for their senior officers and the general Truculence of those political, military, and business commanders.

Note the direct relationship between a leader's stance of aggression and irritability and his ability to command the kind of respect and fear that may produce willing death in subordinates.

The People's Fate Star: You!

The general is the people's fate star,
the master of its safety and
its destiny.
Sun Tzu

The most vital quality a soldier can possess is self-
confidence, utter, complete and bumptious.
George S. Patton

It's all about you.

Sun Tzu talks about the People's Fate Star, doing everything he can, as always, to make you scratch your head and wonder what he's talking about.

What he means is pretty simple, though: War is won or lost
on the quality of leadership. And that means you, right? You,
brother and/or sister. You are the People's Fate Star.

No matter what anybody else says, You, the People's Fate Star,
decide when the battle will be waged. Whatever the big noise
above you is honking about, it will be You, the People's Fate
Star, who decides when to call a halt for dinner. You may even
take a few of your associates with you. It will be You, the People's Fate Star, who decides who will live and who will die, and
the hour of their life and death, particularly at budget review
time.

You are the general. You are the army. You are the planner, the fighter, the leader, the lawgiver, the glue and the grease that makes things run.

It's all about who?

The Warrior Mind

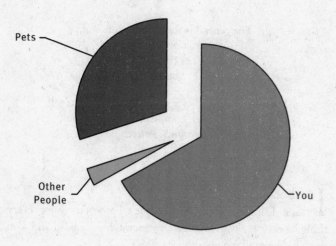

That's right—you. The People's Fate Star.

If you truly know that magnificent fact, people will follow you to the ends of the earth, to death and beyond.

They'd better. Because that's where you're going, pal.

Part Two

Building Your Army

In the operations of war, where there are in the field a
thousand swift chariots, as many heavy chariots, and
a hundred thousand mail-clad soldiers, with provisions
enough to carry them a thousand li, the expenditure at
home and at the front, including entertainment of
guests, small items such as glue and paint, and sums
spent on chariots and armor, will reach the total of a
thousand ounces of silver per day. Such is the cost of
raising an army of 100,000 men.
Sun Tzu

Nuclear war would really set back cable.
Ted Turner

You and Whose Army?

Regard your soldiers as your beloved children and they
will follow you into the deepest valleys. Look on them as
your sons and they will die with you.
Sun Tzu

Wars have never hurt anybody except
the people who die.
Salvador Dalí

For purposes of this discussion, we're going to assume that
while you have intelligence and moxie and good looks, you
don't yet have a working army. This limits your ability to conduct a full-fledged war. And if there's one thing that's invariably
true on this subject, a war that is incompletely fledged is a war
that is almost certainly lost.

You can snipe. You can undermine. You can be a thorn in the
side of the enemy. You can fight courageously unto your lone,
heroic, solitary death. But you cannot wage a victorious war
without some kind of troop. There are, of course, all kinds of
armies, each of which provides certain functions based on its
capabilities:

Kind of Army	Capabilities
A couple of ragtag friends, assorted irregulars	Intelligence, small assassinations
Friends, associates, some key management	Guerrilla warfare, vicious infighting, rearguard actions
Dedicated, loyal staff, close friends, fearful associates	Moderate skirmishes, sieges, short, fierce battles
Modest force of trained regulars, senior staff loyal to your interest, sleazebag spies from the other side who think you may win and want to cover their assets	Good, solid warfare extending over a substantial period of time
Big, mean battalion of warriors who understand your goals and see their own self-interest aligned with yours	Conquest of all competitors, wreaking havoc on all who dare to come within your path
One very old, very mean senior officer who has taken you under his wing	Destroy all your enemies, potentially destroy yourself in the process

As you can see, each type of military force comes with things it can do and things it cannot. One would not, for instance, go at the British Army in an open field with a couple of guys toting rusty muskets. Put those snipers behind a bush, however, and those weedy irregulars can move an empire.

Stop for a moment right now and consider what you have at this time. Then do the opposite of what pacifists everywhere spend their lives doing: Visualize War.

What kind of force do you aspire to? How far away are you from that goal? What should you do to begin?

Making Yourself a General

Train the people. Discipline them.
They will submit.
Sun Tzu

You want loyalty? Get a dog.
My boss

I have more than 100 people reporting to me. Sometimes they're an army. Sometimes they're not. It depends on the task. I guess what it might boil down to is that when I require them to be an army, they might be. If that demand is never made, they're just a good department. That's a lot, during peacetime.

The demands of war on both the leader and his troops are quite different. To engage in true military conflict on your behalf, a group of people must be welded into an army by three key considerations:

1. The consciousness that they are, in fact, an army, and that you are, at least for a limited amount of time, and for a specific purpose, their leader;

2. That there is an enemy who is a danger to the entire ecosystem;

3. That it may be necessary for them to die for the cause, even if the cause is you.

If war should come, I have my doubts whether my department is, in fact, an army *qua* army. It's conceivable, I guess, that a few of my guys would take a small shoulder wound for me. Perhaps a shaving cut, if it was a very bad day and I promised them a long weekend in return. But die? No. I don't expect them to, at this time. And if your army won't die for you, then they're not really an army at all, are they? They're a potential Christmas party.

Why should anybody die for you, anyhow? Would you die for them? Or would you, like most generals, sit on top of the hill as they are mowed down one by one in pursuit of your agendas? Of course you would. That's why you're a potential general. But in the real art of war, that just won't do, ladies and gentlemen. To attract and maintain even the most shoddy, drunken, stupid, and doomed army, you have to be able to do two things:

1. Conduct war without an army, and prove to others that you can do so;

2. In the process, attract others to your flag because most people have no idea what the hell is going on and are looking for some kind of guidance, even from you.

We are now face-to-face with the central issue of the *real* art of war as it is fought on the battlefields of business today: War without an army. Because you are not yet a Bill Gates, with a phalanx of high-paid, exhausted attorneys to do your bidding no matter how madly anticompetitive it might be. You are not a mean, tough bully with unlimited resources like Bill O'Reilly, with enough advertising clout to force the lawyers at NewsCorp to oppose the very First Amendment they are sworn each day to uphold in defense of the rest of their in-house clients. You are not Dennis Kozlowski, with the power to order up a life-sized model of Michelangelo's *David* that pees real vodka.

Perhaps that last is beside the point. There are some things that aren't worth doing, even if you can.

Before you move on to the responsibility of command, Western warrior, you must practice the Art of War without the tools of the genuine Chinese warlord. Without the troops. Without the power over life and death. Without knives, guns, cannons, catapults, bombs, planes, or even all that many dogs of war.

You've got to do it on your own, with nothing but the tools available to the average person with relatively common personal attributes.

War without an Army

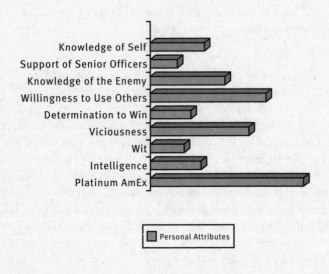

[30]

Using each of these for personal benefit and the destruction of others is what transforms a normal person into a warrior. The ability to get other people to do the same in your behalf transforms the warrior into a general.

Who Are Your Assets?

If victory is too long in coming, the weapons of war
will lose their edge. A protracted war is a drain
on the state.
Sun Tzu

Marriage is the only war where you sleep with the enemy.
Gary Busey

In this very rare case it may be possible that Sun Tzu was
right, and Gary Busey was wrong. Or maybe neither was
right. Let's take Gary Busey first.

Business is a war where you sleep with the enemy every day.
Public Relations people must talk to vicious journalists who say
they're up to one thing when they are in fact in pursuit of quite
another, and be their friends, taking them to meals, feting even
the most fetid of them at endless, weeklong junkets, hobnob-
bing with the very same people who the next day will impale
them with a sharp Gotcha as gleefully as they sopped up free
Chardonnay the night before.

Journalists must stay in touch with sleazy, manipulative Public Relations people who will do everything possible to creep
into their brains and guide their hands, so-called friends who
tell them something isn't happening when later it turns out it
was, and vice versa.

Politicians must talk to each other, knowing that in the breast
of each one beats but one heart, craving but one thing: Me Win.

Doctors must talk to administrators, college professors to deans, rock stars to the networks that put them on the air, except after the Super Bowl.

A lot of husbands and wives sleep together less than the business warrior has to get it on with somebody he doesn't wanna.

In that constant state of warfare, you do have assets. These include:

1. You: you are your own best asset.

2. Business friends, which may be defined as those with whom you talk something other than business at hours that are not traditionally assigned to business. People you have drinks with, or coffee, if you do not drink.

3. Real-world friends, unless you are Martha Stewart, who says something foolish and greedy to her friend only to find it repeated in subsequent testimony.

4. People whose self-interest is identical to your own.

As assets, your permanent and temporary allies, friends, and friendly enemies must be plotted for, sculpted, molded, and sent off to do battle with no particular end in sight. Business is not like war in one critical aspect, unless you're talking about the Hundred Years' War between Germany and somebody else in the 1300s and 1400s. There's no end to it. People die, only to pop up again obnoxiously in another location. You win on Friday, and then get your ass kicked on Monday. So a lot of your assets are only as good as their last engagement.

They, like you, must win almost every time or they lose heart, and new assets must be acquired.

Getting People to Fight:
A Brief Course

When your troops' backs are against the wall they will
fight as if their lives depended on it. Success is preferable
to death, when that is the only alternative.
Sun Tzu

In battle all you need is a little hot blood and the
knowledge that it is more dangerous to lose than to win.
George Bernard Shaw

It is in the deepest part of human nature to avoid pain for
yourself, and not inflict pain on others if you can help it,
unless you are a sadist. Only in business, politics, and the military, each of which is constantly trolling for conflict, advantage,
and gain, is that essentially peaceful human nature violated
every day.

How do you get people to do it? No, desperation doesn't really work, except, perhaps, in those brief, bloody Sun Tzu–style
contests that are begun and ended in a day or so because everybody has only so many chariots.

You need to create the desire to fight the same way you
worked to create love and loyalty in those who have no reason to
feel either. You can do so quite easily—as the volume of idiotic
fighting in this world attests—by answering for each potential
soldier (including yourself) the Five Basic Questions:

1. Why are we doing this? There has to be a reason, even if that reasons is "Because I'm mad!" From the sublime to the ridiculous: one of the things that distinguished the AOL–Time Warner debacle was that nobody on the Time Warner side, let alone outside the company, could understand why a smart dude like Jerry Levin would sell out one of the great companies in the world to a little bunch of pishers. Now it has been explained: there was no reason, other than the vaporous new media imaginings of an overly visionary CEO.

2. What's in it for me? There has to be something good for everybody who fights—survival is enough sometimes, but even better is money, power, or best and least expensive of all, the high regard of those who run his life. "We who are about to die, salute you!" said the gladiators who fought for Caesar as he sat up on the dais eating figs. Why did they die? Why did they salute? Go figure!

3. Will I get hurt? Sure, everybody wants to know that. I want to know that every morning when I wake up and start shaving. What will the day hold? Will the battle be lost or won? And will I get a tummyache? You can't possibly answer this question, so a bit of strategic lying often becomes necessary. During literally every merger I have ever endured, all employees were told it would be good for them. It was almost never good for them. That didn't keep everybody from working day and night to make the deal happen and offer high fives to one another about five minutes before they were shown the door. The lie that everybody will be all right is a good one, in war. You don't need people moping around about the cruelty of fate until they're dead, or at least out of the building.

4. **How long will it take?** In this case, it pays to tell the truth. You don't know. It could be over before teatime, the way Sun Tzu and his fellow sissies would like it to be. Chances are, however, that whatever slugfest you're involved in might go on for days, months, years, or entire careers. I know guys who worked for Pepsi twenty years ago who still won't allow a mouthful of Coke to pass their lips.

5. **Can I have a vacation afterward?** No. After the war comes something even better, my friends—Booty Call!

We'll get into the whole booty aspect of the thing later. Right now, it's time to talk about how you're going to use your cool new weapons and tools. You've got a long way to go before you crack open that bottle of Veuve Clicquot.

Keep the Troop(s) Fat and Happy

Food, ammunition and money—all are equally
crucial. On the move, food is all-important.
In combat, weapons count for more than food.
And an army at rest requires money. Keep your
eye on all three.
Sun Tzu

The first step in having any successful war is getting
people to fight it.
Fran Lebowitz

And to fight it, they need to be fed—in so many ways.

So. Troop #1, as we now know, is You. You are the General, the Army, Special Forces, and the Secret Police all wrapped in one jolly package. You are a Navy SEAL sneaking into the enemy compound in the dead of night. You are a kamikaze streaking down in a ball of flame to take out the guy on the fourteenth floor who is screwing with your agendas. You are Patton with his stick, Larry Ellison with his boats, Hannibal with his elephants crossing the Alps, Diller with his cell phone on the streets of Manhattan. You are all those things, and you need to provide yourself with all the things a good army needs to get going and keep on going until the going is done and it's booty time.

As you go about fighting little battles and creating the proper atmosphere for a good, career-enhancing war, you'll need to treat your army right, in all criteria mentioned by sweet Tzu.

You come first. You also come second. The rest of your army, if any such exists, comes third. Or possibly fourth. After you.

Food

You: Take good care of yourself. Low-carb diets are the rage right now, and they work well because a diet of red meat at all meals (if one considers bacon to be red meat; I do) makes one warlike, particularly when one wants a nice plate of pasta and can't have one. Most important, never miss a meal. It's bad business. And use all meals as a way to muster loyal supporters, except perhaps for breakfast, which often takes place at a time of day where it is virtually impossible to speak.

Your Army: By all means, they should eat. As long as they're available to do what you want when you want it. Discipline is the name of the game for any organization.

You and Your Army: When you're actually fighting or planning an upcoming contest, have either pizza or sandwiches, and don't drink too much. Drinking makes you soft. Wanting a drink makes you feel like fighting.

Weapons

You: Good Lord. You have so many. Your wit! Your good looks! And, most essential, your expense account, which is most useful as a way of seducing new troops onto the plantation.

Your Army: Of course, their expense accounts are their own business, except the ones that have an impact on your budget. Keep an eye on those.

You and Your Army: Everything is a weapon. PowerPoint presentations, so overused in past decades to create an illusion that something smart was going on, are now useful only in a predatory context. That is, aggressive actions can be masqueraded as reasonable using the patina of logic conferred by a graphical treatment.

Disgusting Stuff Masquerading as Acceptable Strategic Idea Because It Is Presented in PowerPoint

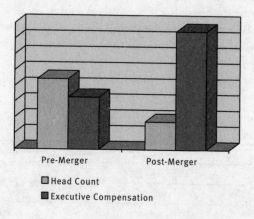

Pre-Merger   Post-Merger

□ Head Count
■ Executive Compensation

There are, of course, many other weapons at your disposal, and we will talk about those later on. But the most effective weapon of all is other people bent to the will of their superiors. Organizations that can produce such people are way ahead of the game.

Money

Sun Tzu says that money is most important during times of rest. That may have been true in ancient China, where places to spend money were between 500 and 2000 miles apart. Today, money is the root of all success. There has to be a lot of money for everybody, all the time, or at least what each member of your so-called army, starting with you, defines as a lot of money.

People at the bottom of your army probably think $100,000 is a lot of money. In the middle, $300,000 is often seen as a benchmark. After that, there are steps, but everybody of consequence wants to think they're worth about a million a year, all in. Then, at the very apex of insanity are the true Generals who only define "a lot" as "more than Eisner or Welch." Everybody has their eye on the rung immediately above theirs, so that's what the booty has to promise, at least in the long term.

You: What you are looking for is a hockey stick in what you could possibly make in the next three to five years. It looks like this:

The Lucky Hockey Stick

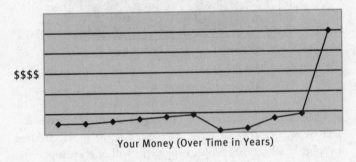

$$$$

Your Money (Over Time in Years)

... with a little downtick for a couple of years of recession during the darkest days of the war ...

Your Army . . . : wants what you want. For themselves. And, of course, for you. Right after that.

Some men may wish to buy presents for their loved ones. Some will prefer to gamble. Others will wish to buy books, trinkets or sweets. The warlord should not be concerned with how a soldier spends his money, as long as it does not interfere with the command.

SUN TZU

As usual, he's got his white silk underwear up on the flagpole. Why not control everything you can? Particularly the gambling part. Unless you're a bookie, you don't want one of your guys heading off to Vegas with his bonus and coming back with snot on his upper lip.

You and Your Army: You are all fighting for the same bold ideal: yourself. That's what makes this business, not religion or government, unless one of those is your business.

Victory! And with it—Wealth! That is the promise you hold out to those who wage war with you, whether that wealth is a new client, subsidiary, or carpeting for your area of the floor. Sometimes it's easier to mount an acquisition than it is to get new office furniture. I'll let you guess which, in the long run, is more important to your future. If everybody at Time Warner had gotten new office furniture and forgotten about the merger with AOL, everybody involved would have been a lot better off.

You Gotta Have Heart

Napoleon said an army fights on its stomach, but that was because they were French. Other nations march on other parts of their bodies. Imagine being a Chinese general in the time of Sun Tzu, having to feed your guys a ton of noodles only to find that half an hour later they were hungry again.

The modern business army also likes lunch, it is true, but it needs something just a little bit more—it needs heart. Whether your squad is enormous or made up of just you and a generally irate assistant, you've got to believe that it's about something bigger than yourself. More difficult for the average warrior/manager is the fact that people have got to believe that you care about them if you want them to lay down their lives for you.

In the first regard—establishing a flag under which an army might be willing to shuffle along, if not to march, exactly—following are some well-known organizations and the general goals they have in the past or are now pursuing in their drive for victory:

ORGANIZATION	GOAL
Ancient Rome	World domination/crush barbarians
Microsoft	World domination/crush Linux
General Electric	Humiliate friends in open meetings/make money
Disney	Protect the chairman
Spanish Inquisition	Wipe out the infidel
The Crusades	Wipe out the infidel
Al Qaeda	Wipe out the infidel
Mel Gibson	Wipe out the infidel
George Washington	Establish the Union
Abraham Lincoln	Defend the Union
Sam Walton	Crush the unions
Dalai Lama/Richard Gere	Free Tibet
My mother	Free Martha Stewart
Average American corporation	Make numbers, safeguard executive bonuses

All laudable goals to be sure, but rather large. In your world, you might want to think about aspirations that, while they continue to motivate people, are a bit more focused. Possibilities in this regard include:

1. Not get yelled at by anybody

2. Have a really good holiday party at the end of the year

3. Beat last year's revenue number, so we can not get yelled at by anybody and have a really good holiday party at the end of the year

4. Take over a few more offices on the floor so we can spread out

5. Humiliate Finance, so they'll leave us alone at budget time

6. Do better than our sister division across town, so that the Chairman likes us better than he likes them and gives us better bonuses

7. Help kids get toys for Christmas, which we can give out at a really good holiday party that has pigs in a blanket and everything

8. Come in #1 in customer satisfaction so we make our number, have a really good holiday party at the end of the year, not get yelled at by anybody, and get plaques

If such goals are communicated to all people in a working situation, they can in themselves create an army, makeshift at first, then more established and solid, used to fighting for the same thing.

But a goal is not enough. The unit, whatever size it might be, must feel that the leader, whatever size he might be, has the best interests of the group—collectively and individually—and holds that concern close to his or her heart, whatever size that might be.

Amazingly, this communication of gemütlichkeit seems to be a tall order for many ostensible generals. Here, then, are methods the insensitive, narcissistic, self-involved, cold, rigid, military, or managerial personality can employ to give the illusion of empathy, compassion, and warmth necessary to generate loyalty and the will to fight in his troops.

* Learn names of people and say hello to them, even when you don't have to. Ways of saying hello include, "Hi, Chuck," when the person's name is Chuck, or "Keep it up, Larry," when, obviously, the person's name is Larry. If their name is neither Larry nor Chuck, you may insert the appropriate one if you can remember it. If you cannot, "Hey, guy!" always is enough to show benign intention, and even "You!" uttered with a knowing smile and a "shooting" index finger and thumb action will do. Any of these strategies convey the message that you care enough about the individual to expend enough energy for a greeting. For some reason this means a lot to people.

* Keep your door open, so that people can come into your office. You may even invite folks in to sit down and talk about themselves. This may create problems in those who have Executive Attention Deficit Disorder (EADD), which may be defined as the inability to pay attention to anything other than one's own thoughts and needs for more than thirty seconds. It's a pervasive complaint that, like many personality disorders, is painless to those who actually suffer from it but inflicts significant discomfort on others. You may work around this heartbreaking disability by making a concerted effort to maintain eye contact with the other person, doing what you can to ascertain what it might be, exactly, that they want, and then quickly either giving it to them or promising that you will "move heaven and earth to make it happen." Remember— an insincere attempt to be sensitive is better than none.

* You may also reach out to others to find out what they think about things. Okay, you don't care all that much, but once again the appearance of caring is almost as good as the real thing.

Several years ago, I worked for a senior officer who had decided that a major acquisition was necessary for us (i.e., him) to stay interested in our primary business. He requisitioned tons of advice from his entire management structure and listened to all of us intently and continually. None of us wanted him to "get it done," as he obsessively described his plan of action. In the end, he did what he wanted to do and we all followed him into battle willingly. His career was killed almost immediately and the rest of us were forced to run into the hills, naked and trembling, to wait for the storm to pass. We still loved him, though, and were happy to serve him. Why wouldn't we? He was such a good listener!

* Begin indoctrinating your potential army on what needs to be done—that is, the need to find the enemy and destroy him, or whatever floats your boat. You won't get loyalty and determination—or anything, for that matter—from people if you don't ask them for it.

* Push the military agenda until people can sing it by heart. As any Moonie will tell you, reiteration is the heart of brainwashing, so stay on message and don't let up. Make sure they're plenty tired. Work them at odd hours. Keep them up late in situations where you can control what they eat and drink and, in the end, what they talk about, find funny, makes them angry. Venues suitable for this important process are meetings, bonfires, bars after work, golf courses, retreats on the beach, and such. The key commitment here is *never to leave the troops alone for too long.* Left to their own devices, they may once again begin to think for themselves. That's your job.

* Be a leader. Wars thrive on clear lines of command. No war can be successful without one. If people are confused about who's running the show, they may start believing they might know how to take better care of themselves than you do. That's a seditious thought that could derail any war you care to conduct.

* Convey a notion of glory that all can share. Empire. Conquest. Survival. Wealth. Market domination. Death to infidels. Grow a big fat carrot that keeps the whole gang running in the same direction.

In short, if you want to be a successful general, try to keep other people in mind, even if for you it's like learning Chinese. Remember it's their war too, if you choose to make it so.

Strike Up the Band

Gongs and drums, banners and flags are means
whereby the ears and eyes of the troops
may be focused.
Sun Tzu

Like many men of my generation, I had an opportunity
to give war a chance, and I promptly chickened out.
P. J. O'Rourke

You have an army now, maybe, if you've been working hard to arrange one, but give those folks half a chance and their natural intelligence will assert itself and they'll quit your war, which, in the end, is not theirs at all, and do what comes a whole lot more naturally—i.e., live in peace.

So in addition to all that we've mentioned in prior chapters, you're now going to ice the cake with a whole lot of hooey that makes war deeper, more meaningful to people, and more fun— the symbols that lend the whole exercise an aura of majesty and importance that wars must have in order to be sustained over a period of time.

These include:

* **A flag or slogan:** In most cases that means a logo that moves the hearts of everybody. But it can also mean a phrase behind which the army can muster. These are not necessarily slogans or banners known to the outside world.

That makes them all the more powerful. When I was a lad, my corporation had a new one every year, including such silly chestnuts as "You Make the Difference," "Together We'll Win," and "We're Building the Best." At first, we blushed at this stuff. After a while, we kind of got a kick out of it. By the end, we were marching along all misty-eyed and proud of ourselves. The human mind and spirit are malleable things indeed, and what we will do if there is love in the air is most alarming.

* **A song:** Not everybody has one, but some fifteen years afterward I remember the lyrics to one of ours. It went like this: "We're building the best/We're passing the test/We're setting our goals/We're taking control/We're building the best." It went to the tune of "I'm So Excited" by the Pointer Sisters. Icky, huh?

* **A uniform:** There's a reason why armies dress alike. To a certain extent, you are what you wear. UPS guys wear those brown outfits with shorts. It doesn't matter. Uniforms are called uniforms because they establish a certain mental uniformity that is required of those who are expected to follow orders uniformly.

* **Rewards for success:** They don't have to be much. A few years ago, our company created pins that were given to people who embodied the spirit of Quality. It was a Q made out of tin. People killed to get them. General Electric has a goofy Six Sigma program that makes people feel juicy about their quality selves. Other companies send people on junkets if they're good, or offer translucent tombstones commemorating battles won in merger transactions. Armies, of course, are expert at this kind of stuff, providing little flecks of metal and ribbon for the

breasts and shoulders of their fighting men and women
that signify the very flesh and blood of life and death. The
object itself makes no matter. It's the getting of it that
drives people to irrational levels of effort and achievement,
or to their doom.

* Parties: They offer fun, relaxation, and, if there is enough
booze around, mutual humiliation and revelation of
genuine self. Have a lot of parties. They build camaraderie
and fool people into believing that the organization cares
more about them as individuals that it actually does.

* Goofing-off time: You can't make people fight every day.
At upper levels, you can encourage a sort of laissez-faire
attitude on Fridays, for instance, that allows the machine
to ratchet down a bit earlier than might be acceptable if
everybody was going by the book. Long lunches for good
warriors are also acceptable in a well-functioning fighting
team. Don't be a stickler about the hours of workers who
will be asked to expire for your purposes at any moment.
It's churlish.

Part Three

The Tao of *Ow*

Dead is dead.
Sun Tzu

Stop. You're killing me.
Anonymous

A Short but Important Chapter

There are five ways of attacking with fire.
The first is to burn soldiers in their camp; the
second is to burn stores; the third is to burn baggage
trains; the fourth is to burn arsenals and magazines;
the fifth is to hurl dropping fire amongst the enemy.
Sun Tzu

The most important thing is to be strong.
With strength one can conquer others,
and to conquer others gives one virtue.
Mao Tse-tung

You gotta wonder about a plan of battle that includes setting fire to people. And makes it the least important
strategic consideration. That said? The big sissy was right.

Let me put it to you this way:

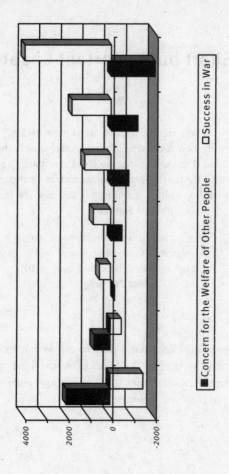

Concern for the Welfare of Other People ■   Success in War □

If you've got a problem with that, you should be reading another book.

Sissy Tzustuff:
Victory without Battle Is Superior

Give them the cold steel, boys!
Lewis Addison Armistead
Civil War, 1863

Just a word about this concept, which is at the deep, drippy heart of Tzu.

The idea is that the highest form of military achievement is found in the commander who can achieve victory without firing a shot. Big points go to those who plan a lot, position themselves perfectly, and wake up the next morning to find themselves masters of the field because the other guy (a) went away, (b) fell down and hurt hisself, or (c) other.

I suppose such things happen. And it's not a bad idea to make sure that you'll have to fight the minimum amount of time, and expend the least amount of resources in doing so, in order to secure what you want. That far we can trot along with this sissy stuff.

But that jujitsu song and dance is a big lie, in the end, and a most unhelpful way to start any campaign. You've got to know that this is war, that war kills people, that those it doesn't actually kill it still hurts quite a bit, and that even if you believe you can get things over with quickly, you probably can't.

I recommend to you, ambitious warrior, the picture of George W. Bush, dressed in fighter pilot's gear from head to toe, beaming on the deck of the aircraft carrier a couple of weeks after U.S. troops embedded themselves into Iraq. Jollity reigned supreme. The war was over. With a relatively small, focused force, we had swiftly seized the high ground and emerged victorious!

PR is important in war. But war is not PR. Those who fail to tell the difference end up either dead or at PR agencies.

There are all kinds of battles. One battle does not a won war make.

And different virtues are needed than those imagined by Sun Tzu and embraced by his fans in the Tao industry.

Tzu Virtues	True Virtues
Wisdom	Aggression
Moderation	Tenacity
Strategic vision	A memory for personal injury like an elephant's
Good supply lines	The ability to hold a major grudge
Knowledge of Tao	Knowledge of Mao
Humility and Grace	A loud voice

Tzu Virtues	True Virtues
Superb command of spatial relationships during a conflict, sensing where moves may be made or avoided to best advantage	The conviction that you are right, always, and a vicious need to eradicate all who oppose you, publicly, if possible
A healthy respect for one's opponent	Paranoia
A dignified command of others	The ability to instill fear
Mysterious communications, featuring lots of poetic metaphors that appeal to nerdy sissies of all stripes	Bluntness approaching tactlessness

You're going to make the other guy go *Ow*. That's all the virtue you're going to need until the war is over. And that could be a good long time. Get that? Now get over it. You've got work to do.

Battle without Victory:
The Way of the Warrior

When you have to kill a man it costs
nothing to be polite.
Winston Churchill

The truth, as opposed to what's been Tzpoon-fed to us at times, is that business warfare is indeterminate in nature, a lot closer to local politics than it is to the grand sweep and weft of hand-to-hand combat. I can't think of the last time that anybody got punched in the nonmetaphorical nose around here.

The average war can take place over the course of months, and perhaps years, and one must learn in the real world to inflict intense *Ow* on other people while still reserving the right to ride up and down in the elevator with them three or four times a day without incident.

Below is a chart mapping the difference between a true armed conflict and the kind that you are likely to encounter in your daily comings and goings.

Arcs of Conflict

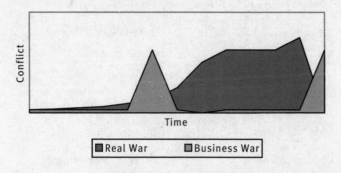

As you see, conventional warfare (dark area) begins in low-level conflict, perhaps an assassination or two, and then escalates into a large conflagration, which may sustain itself over time. When one side prevails, the arc of conflict falls off precipitously.

In the business war (light area), things are different. One must be prepared for a low level of conflict sustained over a period of time, perhaps indefinitely. On occasion, that nagging, aggravating buzz of battle kicks up to lethal proportions, then sinks down again into a dangerous but nontoxic "business as usual" zone. The war goes on and on and on. And there is nothing you can do to stop it except fight in it until either you or it is done.

Look at the length of the campaigns waged by some great warriors of past and present:

Moses Freeing His People	80 years
The Hundred Years' War (ca. 1350–)	100+ years
George Washington	40 years
Abraham Lincoln	5 years (ending in death)
Ho Chi Minh	50 years
Nelson Mandela	30 years (not counting marriage)
Nolan Ryan	32 years
Lew Wasserstein	65 years

Patience is not a virtue in business war. It is a necessity.

Be leery of those who seek to advise you to wage your contests as if you had a howitzer on your shoulder and a grenade on your belt. You don't. And you may have to live in a state of war for your entire career, particularly if you work at a place that favors acquisitions, reorganizations, and McKinsey consultants who earn their living keeping a company in constant turmoil.

Aggression: Accept No Substitutes

The general listens to me.
Use him, for he will definitely win.
The general who doesn't?
You may still use him but he will certainly be a loser.
Get him out of there.
Sun Tzu

Pacifism is fatal to us.
Our goal is to make the enemy passive.
Mao Tse-tung

He was an arrogant little fella, wasn't he? Sun Tzu, I mean. And not that different, when you get right down to it, from Mao. That's why each was good at the art of war, in his day, although their styles were pretty different.

There is no one path to victory. Knowledge of this and that can't hurt. Taking stock of your situation is all well and good. But before we continue, let's repeat the one word answer to the real art of war, Tzu notwithstanding.

It's all you need, and if you have it you have everything. We've mentioned it before. No, it's not Plastic, although God knows you need that. And no, it's not Love, with apologies to John Lennon.

It's Aggression. Raw, amoral, naked aggression and the over-powering will to win each time, every time, all the time. Once you have that, you can add other attributes that will not only aid you in war, they will *create war.*

Come on. Admit it. You want that, don't you? You're a warrior, aren't you? And as such, you have certain characteristics that might be considered flaws in other people, but in you are assets:

* You're never satisfied with your fair share.

* You are swept with great drafts of Greed. Desire. Hostility. Lust. The will to power. Free-floating anger.

* You suffer from a monomaniacal dedication to getting your way, a passion for having things the way you want them.

I know this executive. He shall remain nameless. Throughout his life, he has done very little but fight and fuck. He is not always pleasant. Sometimes he is quite the opposite. Okay, let's be truthful. He's almost never pleasant. But for him, every day is about winning, and by winning I mean two things:

1. Taking more

2. Beating the other guy, in public if possible

Pretty, no. But that's the engine that drives his train, and due to the great psychological disability suffered by all great executives—the inability to be anything but himself, all the time—he has conquered the greater part of the world, and still wants more.

And it all starts with Aggression. Right now, I'm expressing my aggression by attacking Sun Tzu for being a pompous braggadocious bozo. I'm blowing through his passive Eastern equanimity with raw, pure Western muscle. Because you know what? That's what I've got. In fact, it's basically all I've got.

I don't need to practice it. I don't need to study it. I was born with it. And so were you. Because you're not some namby-pamby wimp dressed in a curtain. You're an _____ (fill in your nationality here, even if it is Chinese).

It's good old-fashioned home-style beans. Moxie. Will. Every burgeoning capitalist from Beijing to Barstow wishes he had it too. A lot of them already did, and do. You think Mao tiptoed around like a contemplative monk when he was out to crush his enemies and promote his friends? All right, maybe he didn't have any friends per se, but he certainly had people who he wanted to think were his friends.

No, Mao, who believed revolution grew out of the barrel of a gun, pounded the soft tissue out of anybody in his path. Except when he was running away, as he was forced to do when he was cornered by Chiang Kai-shek in the 1930s. He even did that with great flair, marching his army through the entire length of China so they would live to die for him another day.

Okay, you don't have an army to march through China, but you know what I'm talking about. If you don't, you're probably a sissy just like Sun Tzu and the guys who get so excited about him at Wharton and West Point. If you are, get lost. We don't need you.

The rest of you can continue to the next chapter.

A Nuclear Weapon Is More Effective When It's Exploded Than When It's Used to Hit Someone over the Head

> The best leadership destroys the enemy's plans.
> Next best is to destroy their alliances. After that comes
> the destruction of his army in the field. Worst of all is to
> attack fortified cities.
> **Sun Tzu**

> A handful of soldiers is always better than
> a mouthful of arguments.
> **G. C. Lichtenberg Proverbs, ca. 1700s**

To every battle a proper strategy belongs, and with each strategy comes an appropriate weapon. Sun Tzu gasses on for a while on the subject, but he always comes around to the same wimpy thing, usually avoiding a good, head-on collision in favor of a long trip around the mountain, stopping along the way for a sticky bun and a cup of tea.

You may not be that patient. I know I'm not.

There are a variety of weapons at your disposal even better than sitting around in mufti trying to stay out of trouble.

The following chart demonstrates some of the various weapons at your disposal in the average corporate situation, and their respective utilities in warlike situations in which you may routinely find yourself.

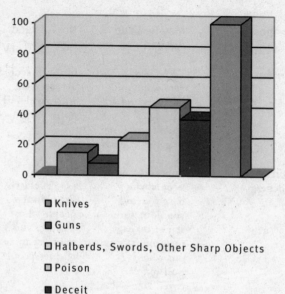

- Knives
- Guns
- Halberds, Swords, Other Sharp Objects
- Poison
- Deceit
- Other People

The number for poison might seem inordinately high to you, but in that category I am including liquor, which can be used by a crafty warrior to completely destroy adversaries who are ripe for that kind of demise. Take your enemy out for an evening in Vegas the night before a big presentation. Keep him out until four in the morning, and make sure he wakes up still drunk and reeking of gin from every pore.

The first weapon, as lame and insubstantial as it might be, is yourself. Of course, you know more about your situation than I do, but here are some handy guidelines, all based on the same principle—a weapon that is highly effective in blowing up an atoll may be a complete waste of time when all you need to do is poke somebody's eye out.

Weapon	May Be Used Against . . .	Not Advised Against
Sarcasm	Peers; people who want your business and are willing to ignore anything to get it; friends	Grumpy senior management with an elevated opinion of itself
Outright rudeness	Subordinates; people who hate you and you don't care, senior management on its way out whose position you covet; Donald Trump	Bosses in power; elderly Republicans; people whose business you want; Japanese businesspeople
Lying	Competitors; peers whose turf you have a hankering for; people of the opposite sex you do not intend to see again, even by accident; people you either hate or love, usually for different purposes; any lawyer but your own	Partners (unless they do it first); people whose opinion you care about; the IRS, SEC, FCC, ASPCA, and other humorless entities

Weapon	May Be Used Against . . .	Not Advised Against
Insincerity	Everyone	N/A
Screaming, jumping up and down, falling to the floor, kicking and pounding feet, other displays of narcissistic petulance	Virtually anyone who cannot defend himself; senior management of acquisition targets worried about their futures after the merger; other pathetic victims	Your boss, your boss's boss, his boss, anybody's boss, Donald Rumsfeld (wouldn't care)
Fists	Those weaker, older, more infirm than you are (ascertain status first); some reporters	Those stronger than you are, bleeders
Truth	Friends, loved ones, people you trust	Everyone else

Obviously, there are many other ways you can hurt and dominate others that have not been mentioned above. Kind words and pretty gifts are very effective against those who crave love and attention. Large, meaty dinners can be used to get concessions out of those poor slobs whose expense accounts are over-scrutinized by accountants. The list goes on.

The Stick, However, Is Less Effective Than a Nuclear Bomb When Dropped from a Height of Several Miles

Plant it good. We don't want him coming out of that
toilet with nothing but his dick in his hand.
Sonny Corleone

The only thing worse than overkill is underkill. Because someone who is underkilled is underdead. Not dead means still dangerous. So if you have a choice between over and under? You know which way to go.

Examples abound of adversaries who were underdead and came back to cause trouble later. They include:

Hamlet's Father: Came back as a ghost and upset Hamlet so badly that, about four hours and five acts later, he killed his uncle, ruining his own stint as King and basically handing Denmark over to a group of very boring Norwegians in scenes usually cut from the play.

Napoleon: Beaten. Sent to Elba. Came back to cause a lot more glorious bloodshed later on. Should have been made completely dead first time around.

Donald Trump: The big doofus just won't stay down.

Slobodan Milošević: He'll be defending himself for years from a comfortable prison suite in some classy European city.

That doesn't sound bad to me, although it's still kind of tough to get ice during the summertime over there.

    Martha Stewart: She'll be back. Count on it.

    So when thinking about how you're going to go forward and do things, plan to err on the side of leaving your opponent overdead. You'll be glad you did.

Size Does Matter

Is that a pistol in your pocket
or are you just happy to see me?
Mae West

There are a number of colossal lies well known to the civilized world, and even elsewhere. "The check is in the mail," for example, is a hoary old chestnut that is still in use everywhere, even though, when it is uttered, it is almost always untrue. There are many others, including some involving human interactions that I cannot repeat here for fear that this book would not then be sold in Wal-Mart.

This point is worth pursuing. I could tell a dirty joke here, not a disgusting one, I assure you, but one that would probably make you laugh. But then the book would not be sold in Wal-Mart, and to tell you the truth, it's just not worth that cost just for a little chuckle from you.

Because it's big, Wal-Mart. It's not just big. It's It. Very. And It knows it.

There's nothing wrong with this. Mick Jagger knows he's big. Jeff Immelt knows he runs a big corporation. Tiger Woods, no matter where he is in the field. Big. These guys walk big. They talk big. They do the dance, because there's no downside in it. And they're all drawing on a power that comes from the feeling that, when the time comes, they will be big enough.

Some people say size doesn't matter. This isn't strictly true. Size in numbers, perhaps, is a nugatory consideration. But the ability to rise to any occasion is perhaps the most critical factor in war.

If you're small, however, don't despair. There are things you should know, and things you can do to make yourself bigger.

First of all, take a deep breath and relax. There. That's better. You can't do a thing when you're tense like that.

Now stretch yourself: No, I'm not talking about that. Meet people. Take on new tasks. Resist the almost inexorable pull into too much definition about yourself. The organization wants to type you, define you, put you in a slot. Reject that utterly. Go places where people don't expect you—with appropriate approvals, of course. Just be where things are going on, whether it's in your discipline or not. Speak when spoken to, but be a good guy to have around. If there's a jump ball, claim it. "Wow," people will say. "I had no idea that Bob could do something like that." If you are Bob, that's good for you.

Width is even more important than length, believe it or not, so broaden yourself. If you're employed, you've got an anticipated function. You've got to blow through that and show that you're as wide as you are long, maybe even making up in width what you lack in length. If you're a numbers guy, surprise people with your all-around grounding in the humanities, for instance. Don't worry if you don't really have one. Neither do they. Read a book about some famous guy and then talk about it in a meeting. Go see a play. You may find something to entertain your pals with other than another atrocious golf story.

Depth, too, is an integral part of whatever size you turn out to be. The great athletes play with emotion. True, much of it is powered by their unwavering belief in their mythological self . . . but so what? Whatever works, you know?

Breadth. With all this? You've got to make it look easy. Saunter when others are running. Breathe deep when others are gasping.

Inflicting Pain
(without the Burden of
Crippling Guilt)

Nothing shall be left to an invaded people
except their eyes for weeping.
Otto von Bismarck

Sit back. This is going to be a very technical chapter.

Unless you are in a highly specialized business indeed, certain weapons will be unavailable for you to use in the process of inflicting *Ow* on other people. Truncheons, for instance, are of limited use to anyone serious about the pursuit of excellence into the twenty-first century and beyond. Spiders that crawl into bed with your adversary and sting him until he cries uncle and dies are hard to find. You can't really use a laser to slice him or her in half.

Those of you in government, law enforcement, or corporate security probably have some extreme unction at your disposal. But most of us make do with less.

Still, the tools available to all of us who are not complete sociopaths are many, rich, and most satisfying, when executed with distinction.

* Insulting: I worked with a very mean, fat guy once who was raised in a certain corporate culture that shall remain nameless, but you probably own its stock, or if you don't,

your mother and your pension fund do. The thing about this fellow was that if you pushed him a little too hard, he was likely to say something that would hurt your feelings. "I don't really see where you have the right to quiz me on this shit," he would murmur, leaning back in his cozy recliner and peering at me from underneath tufty eyebrows worthy of a commissar. "You fucked up that Leventhal situation pretty bad just last week." This would invariably be uttered in front of someone I really couldn't retaliate in front of. Not that I crumbled to the carpet and slobbered salty tears or anything. But it was a hit, a palpable hit, and I still want to give him a wedgie when I think about it.

I don't go in for insulting other people much. It's a small, blunt instrument, and overly personal for me. It also announces your intentions in a most unstrategic way. Finally, it doesn't actually hurt its recipient enough for the risk involved in mounting such an unsophisticated attack.

I'd much rather launch the long-distance precision weapons, often involving highly evolved technology that's fun to use. If I'm going to insult a person at all, which, as I said, is rare, I guess I prefer to do it behind his back, for a variety of excellent reasons that I'm sure you can figure out for yourself.

* Prodding: People, as has been mentioned previously, are often unsure of themselves. You may prod an adversary to do something ill-advised or, as is often the case with enemies, as stupid as you would like him or her to be. Prodding is most successful and appropriate when your adversary is already on the plank and just needs a little nudge to fall over into the water.

* Poking: This is different, more aggressive, than simple prodding. Poking hurts, and must therefore be used only against subordinates, vendors, and others weaker than yourself and unlikely to poke you back. There are a number of venues where a good poke can achieve results, although each comes with a certain danger of immediate reprisal:

Poking: Effectiveness & Danger of Reprisal

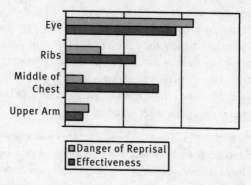

* Kicking: There are only two kicks available to the corporate warrior.

> ➤ Face: while the other guy is down on the ground, covering up;

> ➤ Ass: to get him moving in the direction you want.

Kicking is very, very rude and degrading, and should therefore be used only when all hopes of future peace are dead, or you are in a very bad mood indeed and dealing with someone who wants to get something out of you at some future point in time. In any consideration of kicking, choice of footwear is germane. A small kick with a big boot feels worse than a big one at the business end of a sneaker.

* Goading: Very much like poking and prodding, there is a teasing element in the goad, driving and leading its target into terrain that is unhelpful to his cause. In the 1990s, *Fortune* magazine goaded IBM CEO Lou Gerstner badly with a series of articles that contended that he was a touchy, grouchy bully. This so enraged the head of Big Blue that he proved the magazine correct by canceling all his advertising there for a few years. This is, of course, an example not only of goading but a demonstration of the Pyrrhic victory that can result when the wrong entity is goaded. I'm sure *Fortune* would have liked to have been proven right *and* have kept that ad revenue.

* Undermining: Players in the workplace must live with each other, as we have said. Certain weapons may be deployed, like lead in drinking water, and expected to bear results only in some indeterminate future. In the Bush administration, it was clear from the start that Secretary of the Treasury Paul O'Neill didn't fit into the White House culture very well. In order to destabilize and marginalize him, the administration undermined his position with a variety of little cuts until it became obvious that he was not truly welcome in the war rooms, and he departed. Undermining others takes time and skill and, above all, patience, viz.:

Effectiveness of Undermining Over Time

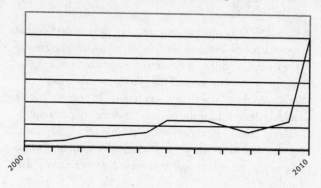

2000   2010

* Humiliating in Public: A particularly effective torture within certain cultures, especially that of General Electric and its many subsidiaries. This is a throwback to the big-dick management philosophies of the 1930s and onward, which were deeply influenced by the prevalence and success of totalitarian systems that were then pushing the boundaries of management dynamism and expertise, looking to leaders who achieved results like Lenin, Stalin, Mussolini, Henry Ford, Louis B. Mayer, and many others.

  The tactic is frowned upon in many companies now as hopelessly out of date. If one becomes known for this style of play, one may quickly find oneself standing out in the street while the nice people are inside the bar having a few collegial drinks.

* Crushing: May be accomplished only by advanced senior officers with major chops. There's nothing more pathetic than the sight of a midget trying to ride a Brahma bull he

has decided to flatten. If you don't have the weight, don't test the freight.

* **Bulldozing:** Is most appropriate not against people, but against issues. Involves heavy consensus-building among the troops, and then a concerted, organized effort to sweep opposition aside. This takes not only good managerial abilities that you may not yet possess, but a big vehicle designed for the purpose and the cooperation of others. That's why mean, stinky people prefer blunt, small, or sharp objects that work quickly, effectively, and without the use of outside people you must convince, manipulate, and trust.

* **Starving:** Useful for controllers and other financial types, who have no compunction about withholding funds from people or projects they despise. Tactic may be employed to great effect against an internal enemy's expense account, making the target mooch off other people for weeks at a time without picking up a single check, no matter how small, like my friend Dworkin, who is the editor of this book.

Other weapons available to those who do not actually tote a flamethrower for a living include: whipping, flaying, burning in effigy in the corporate newsletter, placing the enemy into limbo where people can make fun of him, surprise yelling, screaming, and exhorting, assignment to locations as far-flung, cold, and soul-numbing as Dubuque in the winter.

At the most dramatic end of the spectrum are the huge, emotional weapons that are, in the end, the most effective. They may be employed against enemies both within and outside the company, and never fail to get the job done. I am speaking, of course, of a knife to the heart and the absolutely infallible shot in the head. The first incapacitates the opponent by making him wish he were anywhere but where his spirit is now failing him. The effect of the latter is too obvious to merit discussion. It's hard to operate without a head, even though Westinghouse did it for a couple of decades.

And Now?

Once more into the breach, dear friends!
Henry V

You're armed. You're dangerous. You have the makings of a squad that is, at least, prepared to be tested in battle. And yet . . . and yet . . .

and yet . . . you're a sissy. That's okay. Everyone but madmen is, at the beginning. After a while, however, you're going to have to warm to the work.

Think about wars and other serious conflicts in business, politics, the arts. They are won by the people who most enjoy fighting them. You want that to be you. But it's difficult. You are weighed down, aren't you, by what for lack of a better word I'll refer to as your humanity. This "humanity" is made up of some very discrete and measurable things:

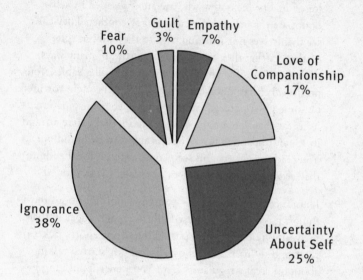

The chart above enumerates the components, in estimated proportions, of what is referred to as "common humanity":

✔ Empathy for people other than yourself (7%): this is difficult to feign, and if you don't have it you're much better off for purposes of what we're talking about. You probably have some feeling for other people, though. Most people do. You'll need to do something about that, not immediately, perhaps, but the time may come when it is a burden to you.

✔ Love of companionship (17%): This, too, can be a hardship if you want to travel light and leave charred earth behind you.

✔ Uncertainty about yourself (25%): Normal people have a lot of it. The lucky few who aren't assailed by self-doubt are the inevitable victors in any conflict. They can't see themselves not winning, and so they win, in spite of the fact that they are often less worthy, in many ways, than the losers. True mental warriors sleep like babies. You, on the other hand, wake in the middle of the night tortured by some poisonous gas seeping out of your imagination. You fear that you are in over your head, that you're a fraud in some fundamental way who is about to be found out. You read the papers and see people exposed for the idiots they are, and you rejoice, because it is not you. Not *yet*.

✔ Ignorance (38%): Face it—you know nothing about most things. Last month, you used salt instead of sugar in that pie you were baking. You put on the wrong sports jacket or scarf and didn't match all day. Somebody started talking about an arcane regulatory issue you were supposed to be on top of, and you weren't—in front of everybody. Fool! Stooge!

✔ Fear (10%): Only crazy people don't feel fear in the face of the carnage of war. You want to be one of those, at least when you're called on to be so.

✔ Guilt about doing bad things (3%): Successful warriors maintain a manageable level of guilt. This is because they have worked out a little synapse in their brains that tells them, when they are doing something wrong, that it's okay because everything they do, in some sense, is right, simply because it is they who are doing it. You probably don't have that button pressed down permanently, although you've felt stirrings of it . . . when you were out of town, or drunk on your ass in Vegas, or in a position of unassailable power in a business situation. . . .

The good news is that you can be free of guilt if you work on it a little. People have done the most terrible things from the dawn of prehistory because they felt they were doing right. This includes:

- ☞ Cain killing Abel
- ☞ The Crusades
- ☞ Slavery in America
- ☞ Suicide bombing by international terrorists (to get back for the Crusades)
- ☞ Michael Jackson having sleepovers with little boys

. . . and so many other awful things, from lynchings supposedly executed in order to protect the virtue of Southern womanhood, to the murder of striking workers by those important philanthropists, Andrew Carnegie and Henry Frick, to the guys who flew those planes on September 11th . . . all thought they were as righteous as could be. The worst things are done not by people who believe they are doing wrong, but by those who are convinced that they walk with the hand of God on one shoulder.

You may not have that capability as yet. But you can, if you're willing to root out your soft, squishy, excessively human center. Don't worry. You'll feel better when it's over.

Part Four

Quashing the Sissy Spirit

If it is not to your advantage, do nothing.
Sun Tzu

Be my brother, or I will kill you.
**Sebastien-Roch Nicholas de
Chamfort,
French Revolution**

Angry You, Invincible You

Why, you. I'll murder you.
Moe Howard

I would like for a moment to consider The Three Stooges. I realize this dates me a bit, because these American humorists' best work was done in the 1930s and 1940s. By the 1950s, they appeared to be nothing but a pack of angry, fat old men poking, slapping, and yelling at each other. I don't know about you, but that's too much like my corporate culture to be all that funny to me.

In their prime, however, the Howard brothers and Larry Fine embodied the hostility, aggression, and mutual need that shape any family, including those that are formed, no matter how temporarily, in the workplace. In each scenario, the toughest, meanest, most abusive and least sympathetic individual is selected to run the group and impose the kind of discipline that is excessive, emotional, irrational when need be, and successful.

The world of the stooges, although hopelessly downscale, is reminiscent of one in which many of us have worked for a living. The three are invariably assigned to do something that they are inadequate to perform, because they are stooges. They must, however, come through, or there will be hell to pay from bosses (or spouses) that are very disagreeable. They show up and eventually get the job done, primarily because the most aggressive one—Moe, with the bowl haircut and the small mustache that evoked both Charlie

Chaplin and Adolf Hitler—goads, bullies, and physically abuses the other two stooges into some form of compliance with the requirements that are at hand. A lot of the time he fails, of course, and everybody ends up in some kind of hot water.

The main focus of each story is how each stooge suffers—the atmosphere is suffused with anxiety—and the ubiquitous rage and fear that enable the three to manage in spite of their stoogeness.

The subordinates—Larry, Curly, Shemp, and the depressing Curly Joe—suffer directly at the hands of their superior, Moe. He, in his turn, suffers when they inadvertently hit him with a board, etc., and even when he isn't injured physically, he spends a lot of the time in a high level of frustration, as do many senior managers. This frustration circles back again and is expressed as an even more extreme form of rage until he is so apoplectic that a stroke is not out of the question. I've seen executives in exactly that frame of mind more times than you can shake a stick at. I saw one so mad one time I thought his eyes were going to explode from his head the way Ronny Cox's did at the end of *Total Recall*.

This is too much like the average workplace to be devoid of meaning for us as warriors. The lessons, even for those who do not consider themselves stooges, would appear to be simple but important:

1. No pain, no gain: Each stooge transaction is achieved only after incalculable suffering, which is funny to us because it is not ours but is reminiscent of ways that we have felt in the past.

2. There is tremendous power in anger.

It is this last quality—the capability to generate and act upon great wells of anger—that makes the difference when war comes. Warriors who do not fight with anger are doomed. This is in direct opposition to Mr. Tzissy, who counsels wisdom and sanity and chides the angry general with threats of abject defeat.

Other than patience and a hollow leg, anger is the single most important personal attribute that a warrior can possess. On a business terrain, the player who fights without anger is at a distinct disadvantage, because the real guns out there are furious all the time, and are truly happy only if they are stomping on the face that they have just torn from the bleeding skull of their despised adversary.

You have a lot of really successful people you can look to for inspiration in this regard.

Angry Managers Now and in the Past

MANAGER	SOURCE OF ANGER
God	Sodom
Atilla the Hun	Non-Huns
Richard the Lionhearted	The Infidel
Henry Ford	The Elders of Zion, Chevrolet
Joseph Stalin	Rearguard Leninists, Trotskyites, trade unionists
Douglas MacArthur	Communists, Japanese, Chinese and Koreans, Harry Truman
Richard Nixon	Enemies
Walter Yetnikoff	Lawrence Tisch
Rupert Murdoch/ Ted Turner	Each other

MANAGER	SOURCE OF ANGER
House Republicans	Blow jobs for presidents
Michael Eisner	Jeffrey Katzenberg, Roy Disney, kids who don't seem to be going to his movies, a lot of his shareholders, unclear feelings about Michael Ovitz, the guys over at Pixar, for the moment
Martha Stewart	Feds in bad suits
Jack Welch	Morons who question his judgment
Congress	Dirty television programs like *Friends*

Think of your own managers. Aren't they always exercised about something, often quite stupid and seemingly inconsequential? The truth is, it doesn't matter what they're angry about. It is the anger itself that keeps the gears of war grinding smoothly.

Go. Search deep within yourself. And, if you are truthful with yourself, and patient, waiting for it to make itself visible to you, you will, in whatever time it takes you, find your button.

Finding Your Button

You can't touch this.
M. C. Hammer

Everybody has a button. The problem with you is that yours is flabby.

Perhaps you have read a bit too much nontzense on the evils of anger, or are too mild-mannered by nature. Either way, you're scheduled on the 4:19 to Disaster if you don't toughen up and start that big old furnace that's sitting in your basement, waiting for a match.

In the last chapter, we looked at some subjects that I offered in order to help you achieve a state of warlike irritation, not knowing you very well at all and, frankly, having no desire to do so. I hope you've chosen a good thing to be angry about by now. You should have.

If all else fails, you may choose "Anyone who opposes me on any subject, no matter how small." It works for a lot of very successful people. Most of the big guys I know don't need any more than a small, negative observation in a newspaper to set them off for three or four hours. You want to be like that.

Once you have a topic that gets under your skin, you must do what successful warriors do and turn that annoyance into a white-hot coal of anger that can be doused only by the death of your enemies.

This you can do in a five-step program of anger management—not in the sense that term is usually employed, of course. In your case, we're going to manage your anger *upward*, so that it may be used as a weapon in itself, and as fuel for other weapons that are relatively toothless without it.

Producing Anger: A Five-Step Program

Step One: Cogitation: You've already done a fair amount of this in selecting the thing that peeves you. But don't stop at one. Targets for your anger are like potato chips. Once you start eating them, you want more. The rush of adrenaline and bile provided by a good bolt of anger is addictive, and like any addictive substance, your tolerance and need for it will grow as you become more inured to smaller doses.

Note: The best time for cogitation is either late at night or early morning. Both will set you up for an angry new day on the morrow without getting in the way of your daily wartime duties.

Step Two: Marination: A decent anger starts small and then grows deeper and richer as it is marinated inside you over time. If you've done your cogitation, you've got this thing moving inside of you, seeking release in the form of action. But anger that is acted upon too soon may taste green, be rather hard to chew, and give you a stomachache afterward. Unripe anger can result in stupid, violent acts that are lacking in sustainable force over time. A truly functional anger that can quash your sissy spirit must be cultivated and not expressed before it is ready.

Fluids in which you may marinate your anger include:

* Bile

* Blood

* Vodka, Scotch, gin, assorted cordials

* Latte with a "depth charge" of espresso (West Coast)

Step Three: Frustration: Major-league warriors go around all the time in a state of high aggravation. This is because they always have a variety of angers working, in varying stages of marination. Some are righteously plump and ready to pop. Others are just being immersed in the proper solution for steeping. Those that are closest to maturity begin to seethe and bubble, calling out for action from the depths.

The danger in walking around with too much unexpiated frustration is that it turns you stupid. Symptoms of impacted frustration include irritability at the wrong people, violence toward the wrong people, increased alcohol consumption, irrational yelling, kicking the family pet or random delivery people, road rage, etc.

While a low stew of frustration is necessary to feed your warlike spirit, frustration must be controlled to do you any good.

Step Four: Machination: I don't want you to think that war is all a big fat downer. It's not. Most of the time it can be quite a lot of fun, particularly for the generals. Many of you reading this book are sadomasochists who have enjoyed Steps One to Three already. For the rest, here's where the enjoyment phase starts as you begin to plan, foment, wheedle, organize, and set up the actual campaign against the enemy.

This step is enormously important, because those who skip right from Step Three to Step Five often find themselves hoisted on the wrong side of the petard, whatever that is. Planning is also quite important in maintaining the kind of anger you need to keep your sissy spirit in check. Many of you are relatively healthy people who find it difficult to keep a proper level of homicidal rage cooking along nicely. You tend to get less angry over time, and to forgive people their trespasses against you as you would have them forgive yours against them, that kind of thing. This has a direct and negative impact on your success during wartime.

Warriors Grow Their Anger—and Achieve Success

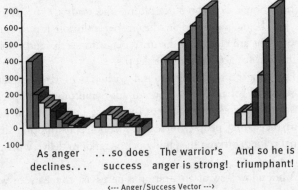

As anger declines... ...so does success The warrior's anger is strong! And so he is triumphant!

<--- Anger/Success Vector --->

The only way to keep a suitable level of anger over time, especially when matters assume their correct proportion—as they will, for most sane people—is to plot, scheme, and otherwise entertain yourself with scenarios that involve the destruction of your enemy. As you are planning, keep in mind that the better the plan, the more likely its success.

Step Five: Mastication, Defenestration, Devastation: This is the hardest part. The details of actual warfare are horrible and involve tremendous suffering, even for you, no matter how lucky, prescient, careless about other people's feelings, and attentive to your own that you might be. We will be discussing the actual terms of engagement in a little while, but if you don't keep your anger up during this time of the most intense battle, the repercussions for you could be dire, involving loss of will, stomach lining, and, worst of all, hair.

True warriors sustain their rage simply by thinking about how their adversary actually has the temerity to oppose them. They also nurse wounds and grievances all out of proportion to the severity of the actual insult. This gives them power.

Abandoning Sympathy

On the day they order their men into battle, the officers'
shirtfronts are moist with tears, except for those who are
reclining, whose tears stain their cheeks.
Sun Tzu

"I weep for you," the Walrus said:
"I deeply sympathize."
With sobs and tears he sorted out
Those of the largest size,
Holding his pocket-handkerchief
Before his streaming eyes.

"O Oysters," said the Carpenter,
"You had a pleasant run!
Shall we be trotting home again?"
But answer came there none—
And this was scarcely odd, because
They'd eaten every one.
Lewis Carroll

Anger is not enough, in the end, to squash the spirit that in-
habits all but the most sociopathic breast. As the sage
poinTz out, it is difficult for the officers on the day when they
send troops to their deaths. Those that are sitting moisten their
shirtfronts. Those who are lying down stain their poor little cheeks. This does not stop them, however, from issuing the
orders.

And it shouldn't stop you, either.

If you're going to enjoy a life of warfare, you can't go shedding bitter salty drops every time you crack open an oyster.

Even generals have to eat.

Rejoicing in His Weakness: A Brief Quiz

Now you don't talk so loud.
Now you don't feel so proud . . .
about having to be scrounging your next meal.
How does it feel?
Bob Dylan
"Like a Rolling Stone"

Q:When you see somebody more pathetic than you are, what is your reaction? Do you:

a) *Feel very bad for the fellow, and seek to help him on his thorny path?* The guys at Enron must have felt this way about their employees and shareholders, knowing what they knew about their rotten, fraudulent company, but they never acted on it. They kept it to themselves. That must have been quite a burden for them, and I bet they feel bad about it now.
b) *Realize that business is business but do your best to help the loser out with a couple of bucks if you have the opportunity?* When my company divested its flute-reamer division a couple of years ago, a whole bunch of middle management got wasted. On their way out the door, they got some very nice parting gifts, though.
c) *See the guy's strong points and attempt to create a friend and ally in this gibbering homunculus?* It can be done. Jack Welch saw something

in Jeff Immelt that spoke to him. Howard Stringer even saw
something in Andy Lack.

d) *Ascertain whether the guy is a friend or an enemy.* If he's in the green
zone, you shore him up, but that's not as interesting as if he's
a weenie, in which case you thank the Lord for sending you a
dork for an enemy.

A:

a) *You're a nerd.*
b) *You're in Human Resources.*
c) *Your subscription to the* Harvard Business Review *is in the mail.*
d) *Bingo.*

Busting a Move

Await chaos with calm, silence to prepare for noise.
This will bring order to your spirit.
Sun Tzu

Just one of your balls, Smitty. You can live without it.
That's why they gave you two.
Lee Marvin
The Big Red One

There's a lot of lurking around in the original *Art of War*. Generals assess. Troops search high and low for the proper venue for further waiting and strategic skulking. They attack, eventually, but only when victory is assured by a variety of criteria.

But lurking has its limitations.

Side Effects of Overlurking

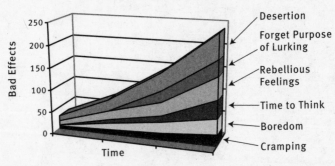

Worst of all, perhaps, is the fact that extensive strategic skulking, lurking, hovering, etc., all build the strength of the debilitating sissy spirit within you. This doesn't mean that you won't fight eventually, not necessarily. It means that you'll wait for things to develop before you make up your mind to act. You will develop a *penchant for inaction* that feeds on itself until you're one of those guys who needs corporate permission before you can scratch yourself. Anybody who has ever dealt with Japanese executives (except for those of the very highest rank) or the development people at HBO will recognize this phenomenon.

At the top of such organizations are one or two warriors who make all the calls. In the middle, well, it's hard to figure out what those people do to earn their money. Making decisions and taking steps are not among their daily activities.

Great warriors may also lurk before they leap—but they have the capability, the *need*, to bust a move and make something happen. Sometimes these are stupid, brutal, or unnecessary things, but you can't say they didn't make them happen.

Like this:

WARRIOR	ACTION
Moses	Parted Red Sea, made flood
Pharaoh	Drove into the flood
Howell Raines	Flooded the zone
Nero	Set fire to Rome
William the Conqueror	Invaded England
Samuel Adams	Dumped tea in Boston Harbor, made beer (?)
Charles Lindbergh	Flew across Atlantic/ supported Adolf Hitler

WARRIOR	ACTION
Bob Dylan	Went electric
Guy in Tiananmen Square	Faced tanks
"Chainsaw" Al Dunlap	Fired lots of people/made lots of money
Jeff Katzenberg	Got mad/formed SKG

I'm sure you can think of other individuals, each of whom, for reasons good or bad of their own, cast their fate to the heavens and took the one big step that separates yesterday from tomorrow.

In that moment, they left their sissy spirits behind.

Part Five

Enemies

This is the end, beautiful friend, the end.
Jim Morrison

My Enemy, Myself

I have only ever made one prayer to God,
a very short one: "Oh Lord, make my enemies
ridiculous." And God granted it.
Voltaire (1767)

What is an enemy, I mean, all kidding and poetry aside? It's an entity very much like you that you want to kill. You must understand that thing on the other side of the barbed wire, think long and deep about its weaknesses and its strength, and then hurl yourself at it like a dog on its own reflection—possibly with the same result.

This notion—that your enemy is pretty much you with a different suit on—is an obnoxious one to many people. It's far easier to imagine that the enemy is a troll and a monster when one is planning to blow him up.

The good news for those who choose to delude themselves in this regard is that our enemies often comply with our desires and act as idiotic, selfish, and demented as we wish. Of course, we appear exactly that way to them, too. But let that pass.

How your adversary appears ridiculous to you is important, for it is in those excesses that his or her Achilles' heel may be found, even if it is nowhere near his shoe.

Let me give you an idea of what I mean.

Warrior	Enemy	How Enemy Appears Ridiculous to Them
Augustus Caesar	Mark Antony	Sex-crazed moron
George Washington	George III	Pompous, snuff-sniffing sissy-boy
Napoleon	Everybody but France	Not French
V. I. Lenin	The Czar	Inbred, overfed, disgustingly opulent vampire, sucking off the working class
John Lennon	J. Edgar Hoover	Fat, corrupt fascist who probably wears women's underwear
J. Edgar Hoover	Martin Luther King	Sexed-up troublemaker in bed with Robert Kennedy
Richard Nixon	Just about everybody	Commies, homosexuals, Jews, other Democrats

Warrior	Enemy	How Enemy Appears Ridiculous to Them
Tupac Shakur	Biggie Smalls	Big fat doofus
Biggie Smalls	Tupac Shakur	Middle-class kid dressed up as gangsta wannabe
House Republicans	Bill Clinton	Sex-crazed moron
Fred Durst / Christina Aguilera	Christina Aguilera / Fred Durst	Bimbo with no talent
Al Franken	Newt Gingrich	Sex-crazed moron

In some cases, as you can see, the warrior made a proper evaluation of his adversary. In others, an underestimation resulted in a surprising loss for someone who expected an easy ride.

What makes sense, in the end, is to find your enemy ridiculous and eminently defeatable, while at the same time secretly taking care to assess the reality of the situation.

Reality and fantasy, mixed. This is the greatest ally of any warrior. Knowing the right proportions may spell the difference between victory and defeat.

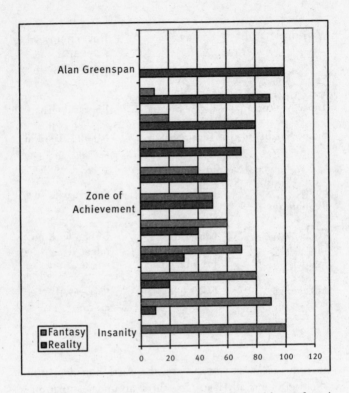

Let's take a look at the enemy realistically, and how, if you're not a complete weenie, you can deal with each and every kind.

A word of caution. I don't have a lot of time. I have a real job where I'm up to my ass in alligators. What follows is a complete and total treatment of every enemy you're likely to meet in the course of your career, with an appropriate approach to each.

The Small Enemy

Uh-oh. Wan outta piddies.
***Tweetie Bird, watching Sylvester fall into
the abyss after peeling his enemy's final pinkie
from the rope that was holding him up***

A warning that is probably the best piece of advice you'll ever get in business: watch out for short men. Short men, which I define as men who must look up to look down, are extraordinarily powerful adversaries. They have been fighting their height all their lives. The ones who have conquered that psychological impediment can run roughshod over just about anybody.

The same thing, by the way, can be said for short women who make it, as anyone who has seen Ruth Westheimer work a party can tell you.

The basis for this assessment is not philosophical. It is empirical, at least on my part. My first boss was short, and was a complete Nazi. My second boss was a short woman, and she could crush walnuts with her molars. I have worked for many, many magazine editors. Most of them have been short, and the ones who weren't short thought they were.

I will confine myself to great leaders in world history who were short to make my point, although there is a plethora of short moguls around in every industry, and the ones who aren't short are often fat. We'll deal with the fat guys later.

They don't do as well as the short ones, because they often die earlier.

List of Small but Formidable People throughout History

1. The Black Prince, a famous knight of the Middle Ages, whose armor would fit Gary Coleman

2. Alexander Pope, English poet—4 ft. 6 in.

3. Victoria, British queen—5 ft.

4. John Keats, English poet—5 ft. ¾ in.

5. St. Francis of Assisi, Italian saint—5 ft. 1 in.

6. Henri-Marie-Raymond de Toulouse-Lautrec, French painter—5 ft. 1 in.

7. Honoré de Balzac, French novelist—5 ft. 2 in.

8. Nikita Khrushchev, Soviet leader—5 ft. 3 in.

9. Marquis de Sade, French soldier, writer, and sadist—5 ft. 3 in.

10. Charles I, British king—5 ft. 4 in.

11. James Madison, U.S. president—5 ft. 4 in.

12. Pablo Picasso, Spanish painter—5 ft. 4 in.

13. George "Baby Face" Nelson, U.S. gangster—5 ft. 4¾ in.

14. Hirohito, Japanese emperor—5 ft. 5 in.

15. Lawrence of Arabia, British soldier and writer—5 ft. 5½ in.

16. Napoleon Bonaparte, French emperor—5 ft. 6 in.

17. Joseph Stalin, Soviet political leader—5 ft. 6 in.

18. Tutankhamen, Egyptian king—5 ft. 6 in.

Current power players for the short team include most famous male actors, tiny titan media mogul Si Newhouse and so many others, consultant, alleged war criminal, and *bon vivant* Henry Kissinger, and comedian Jon Stewart. I employ these examples only because none of them seem capable of doing me harm in the near term, and none are likely to read this book, even the living ones.

Shortness of stature is not the only consideration. Of equal concern to you should be small to medium-sized managers who hate your guts, and most important, assistants (who used to be called secretaries) who plot among themselves to take you down. If you have actually been stupid enough to alienate the people who work for you and your peers and bosses, then it's possible there's nothing I can do for you.

SMALL ENEMY TACTICS

✔ You are holding a raw egg. Don't worry, it's got its shell on it. It's not messy. Yet. Regard the egg in your hands. You have to get it to Khartoum, over rough and rugged terrain.

✔ There are other people along on your dangerous journey, skulking guys with eye patches and black do-rags, or whatever it is that Steve Van Zandt wears. They want to take your egg, for reasons of their own. You must keep possession of the egg all the way to Khartoum or you have failed.

✔ At the same time, you must pursue your everyday duties, which are important—in fact, even more important to you than this worthless egg you are being forced to tend.

✔ The trip to Khartoum continues. Perhaps you will never get there!

✔ Eventually, you do. Khartoum! Romantic, exciting capital of something or other. Where is it, anyhow? It doesn't matter. You have arrived.

✔ You take your egg to the appointed place where it was expected, and, arriving there exactly on time, you break it on the pavement and watch it fry on the sidewalk. And a good thing. What a pain in the neck that egg was!

The Big Enemy

Gee, you're the biggest Jew I've ever met.
Ted Turner to the 6'3", 245-pound Rick Kaplan,
when he was hiring Kaplan to run CNN

Physical size is not an insignificant consideration in contests between human beings. Let me tell you a little story. I don't think it's all that unusual.

Once upon a time, there was an extraordinarily insufficient senior officer. The company was in terrible shape at the time, and this fellow did very little to ameliorate the situation. He liked consultants, I'll say that for him.

Bob's chief assets were twofold:

1. He said very little.

2. He was very tall.

At meetings, he would sit brooding at the head of the table, his Lincolnesque legs stuck out in front of him, leaning back in his recliner, listening, or not listening, you couldn't really tell. At the end of the meeting, he got up and stood, looming over everybody until, tired of waiting around for anything more than pleasantries, the group broke up and frittered off. And Bob had got through another meeting.

He did this act until a group of shorter people swarmed

around his ankles and brought him down. I don't think he really cared, when the end came. He sauntered off into the wilderness, confident that there would be a place for a tall man in another venue. As, indeed, there was. And now he's busy and successful being tall elsewhere, to their consternation, I am sure.

BIG ENEMY TACTICS

✔ A giant lives in a tower on the far side of the woods, spending his days eating the bones of commoners, drinking as much wine and mead as he can pour down his gullet, and counting his gold. There is no reason for you to go there unless one of two things is happening: (1) you have been summoned by the giant either to entertain him or to be eaten by him, or (2) you have gotten to the point where you and your compatriots believe you can bring the giant down.

✔ You stay to yourself, do your job, keep your nose clean, make friends. No one person can defeat a whole giant.

✔ One night, when the giant is sleeping off one of his magnificent displays of excess, you are awakened by Thor, a dwarf who most closely serves the giant when he is in a busy vein. "Are you with us or against us?" he says.

✔ Together, you and your crew of dwarfs, elves, men, women, and even a few orcs swarm into the castle that houses the board of directors that controls the tower. The next morning, either the giant is gone or you are.

✔ When giants leave, by the way, they often take a lot of their gold with them, along with a couple of chickens and the occasional ham. Ask Dick Grasso and the board of the New York Stock Exchange about the rationale behind that.

A Last Word about Size

I don't like you 'cause your feets too big.
Fats Waller

In the last couple of chapters I may have given the impression that sheer height is the only determinant of size. It isn't. Other factors include:

* Rank

* Quality of attire

* Physical beauty or conspicuous lack of it (as a positive)

* Sex appeal

* Level of aggressiveness

* Ego—that is, an inability to perceive oneself as having the capacity to be wrong

Rank is most crucial, but not how you might think. On the next page there is a chart describing the level of discomfort various players can inflict on your situation, if you get on their wrong side, whether that side be tiny or grotesquely Trumpian in its dimensions.

You will notice that the greatest depredations can be visited on you not, as you might think, by the middle management that you end up fighting with every day. The true, abiding danger to you, if you are a twerp, is from the service people who keep the machine running, workers who used to be called secretaries but are now happier when you call them assistants. Most of these assistants you don't even see every day because they work for other people, but they know who you are, believe me, what you eat, what you drink and when, how your expenses pan out, and other minor things like that, up to and including who you're in love with, if you know what I'm talking about.

On the other end are a few people you seldom see either, who can hurt you without knowing you at all if the spirit of economy and frugality is upon them.

Power to Annoy

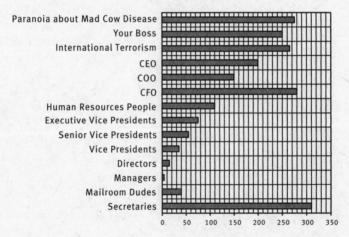

GENERIC SIZE TACTICS

✔ Forget about all that executive Tzustuff for a second. If you don't take care of the secretaries and the guys in the mail-room, you'd better just call it quits right now.

The Fat Enemy

Try the veal. It's the best in the city.
**Captain McCluskey to Michael Corleone,
right before Michael shoots him in the throat**

I'm not a fat person, but I could be if I wanted to, and possibly even if I didn't. I've got the appetite for it. As a young lad, I used to eat a pound of pasta in one sitting, and then have an ice cream sandwich. After a night of working in college, I liked to go out with pals for a pitcher of beer and a sixteen-inch sausage pizza, just for me. I weigh thirty pounds more standing right here before you than I did then and eat 146 percent less. Life is unfair.

People who want to be fat are always fighting not to be. This makes them very jolly. But beneath that jolliness, ladies and gentlemen, lurks a hardened, suffering, ravening beast, hungering, hungering for . . . more.

That's why fat people, like short people and very tall people, are dangerous and must be watched with great care. One minute they're honking up a storm, laughin' and scratchin' like the world is an oyster and you are the pearl in it, and the next they're asking you if you want to eat that pickle. Things go downhill from there.

Before we get all strategic on it, let's answer a key question: what is "fat"? In business terms I would define it as follows:

- More than twenty-five pounds overweight by any rational standard.

- Parts of you are squeaking out of your clothes a little, and you have trouble keeping your shirt or blouse tucked in.

- People call you "big guy," if you're a guy. I'm not sure if there's a female counterpart. They mean it as an affectionate sobriquet, but it isn't. When people use it on me, it makes me feel like Chris Farley, even though I am not, as I said, one bit fat. So if you're one of those people who like to do that to burly people, cut it out.

- You're thinking about food right now. Bacon or sausage, probably, if you're a guy. Ice cream, I would guess, or crème brûleé, if you're a woman.

- You're greedy for other people's turf, and don't have anything against eating it if it's put in front of you.

Fat people make excellent friends, and absolutely despicable enemies, because, like some other oppressed groups, they have hidden reservoirs of anger.

Capacity for Anger

Larry David	███████████████████
Enron Employee	███████████████
Iraqi Shi'ites	████████████████
Bill O'Reilly	███████████████████
Fat People	██████████████████████

Jolliness ------> Towering Rage

And like any people who are subject to enforced jocularity over a period of time, once angered, this is a group that isn't afraid to throw its weight around, making a chronic social liability into a real asset in times of struggle.

FAT ENEMY TACTICS

✔ You are fond of your new pit bull, Chuck. Chuck is not like other pit bulls. He's friendly and sweet. People marvel at what a good disposition he has.

✔ One day, Chuck is out on his own when he gets hungry and displays a whole new side of his personality, killing and devouring a small vice president who made the mistake of poking him with a stick.

✔ After this unfortunate incident, it becomes clear to you that Chuck seems interested in the fleshy part of *your* leg between the ankle and the back of the knee.

✔ Chuck's a problem now, to you personally. There's no chance he's going to go back to the nice little puppy you played with and trusted. There is, obviously, only one thing you can do.

✔ You feed Chuck. Omelets and bacon and big fat steaks at noon and a nice chop with fries at dinnertime, with a couple of drinks anytime he wants them. Whenever the dog looks up long enough to catch his breath, you've got a nice, fatty bone to throw him.

✔ After a few months of constant force-feeding, Chuck is so stuffed he can barely get around. He couldn't bite another executive if his life depended on it. People kind of wince when they see him roll by.

✔ In the fall, around budget time, you quietly load Chuck into the dogcatcher's wagon and sign the papers committing him to a nice long stay at the pound.

The Skinny Enemy

A wise general eats his enemy's food.
One of his chickens is worth twenty of mine.
Sun Tzu

A hungry man is an angry man.
English proverb

"Y on Cassius has a lean and hungry look," Shakespeare wrote of the one conspirator who stabbed Caesar not for Rome, but to satisfy his own hunger for power and vengeance. Something about a guy who eats but is never truly fed is unnerving to people.

This is often unfair. There are as many prejudices and antagonisms against skinny people as there are against fat people. They just look better both in their clothing and without it.

As a potential fat person, I admit to a visceral mistrust of people who don't have enough heft to them. Of special annoyance to me are the ones who complain how they have to drink milk shakes and eat onion rings all the time to keep their body weight up. I suspect this is being said to destabilize me in some way, although that's not a very difficult task at this point in time.

Skinny people, like short people, tall people, and fat people, need to get their asses kicked now and then. In this case, however, that may be more difficult than one might expect. It's hard to kick a small, moving target.

Let's look at what we mean by skinny:

- ☛ Seat of pants appears relatively empty;

- ☛ Always buttons middle button of jacket to conceal lack of girth;

- ☛ Never seems to have enough to do, and eyes your platter greedily when he thinks you're not looking.

This last point is important. The skinniness we're considering here, as you no doubt have perceived from prior segments in this chapter, is not merely physical. It has just as much to do with a player that is perpetually ravening, and has no scruples about eating your lunch if nobody else's is around.

SKINNY ENEMY TACTICS

✔ You are in a boat on a long, broad river, moving slowly downstream. With you is another. He or she is all skin and bones, and there is one loaf of bread between you.

✔ As the days go by and the food grows shorter, your companion becomes very grouchy, and you notice him discreetly salivating over your share of the rations.

✔ One night, as he sleeps, you quietly steal a piece of his bread, but so small a piece that he does not notice, and eat it immediately. This fortifies you, and while it does not immediately hurt him, it makes him ever-so-slightly less potent a potential adversary in the future.

✔ As each night passes, you acquire ever-increasing portions of his store, while keeping a tight eye on your own. He has a choice now: He can take you on head-to-head, but this would take strength, and he's so hungry!

✔ After a week, the mad, emaciated creature attacks you in the boat. After a short struggle, you easily overpower him and, taking the last of his food, throw him overboard, where he is swept downstream and over the falls.

✔ The moment he is gone, you head for shore, where you book a room at the St. Regis, have a shower, and head for Sparks, where you have a forty-eight-ounce T-bone and a baked potato with all the fixin's.

The Weak Enemy

Soldiering, my dear madam, is the coward's art
of attacking mercilessly when you are strong, and
keeping out of harm's way when you are weak.
That is the whole secret of successful fighting.
Get your enemy at a disadvantage; and never,
on any account, fight him on equal terms.
George Bernard Shaw

For purposes of this discussion, let's do what Richard Nixon always enjoyed, and make one thing perfectly clear: there are no weak enemies.

If you believe you have one, you're about to fall into the tar pit where, in a couple of million years, people will find your fossilized remains with a surprised expression on their face.

Not that some opponents are not weak. It's just that weakness, in the right hands, conveys a certain strength. Weakness forces a warrior to express his aggression in other, more unexpected ways, some of which can be very successful indeed, particularly against an overconfident adversary.

Here are some "weak" enemies who have succeeded in wiping out "strong" adversaries over the years:

* David, King of Israel, over Goliath, a giant who worked for a group of art critics called the Philistines.

* The Continental Army under George Washington, which defeated the mightiest army in the world by inventing guerrilla warfare

* Ho Chi Minh, who defeated the armies of both France and the United States in his drive to create a unified Vietnam that is only slightly less oppressive than one would expect it to be

* The 1969 Mets

All people have power. That power can be expressed in a variety of ways by those who are angry, or ambitious, or determined to make you feel sorry for taking them too lightly.

WEAK ENEMY TACTICS

✔ You wake up one morning to find a small pack with a five-pound fruitcake in it strapped to your back. A voice tells you that you may not take off this small burden, except to sleep, for the foreseeable future. "What's the big deal?" you think to yourself. "It's not even five pounds." "Fine," says the voice. "Just don't let it out of your sight. It was a present. I'll be back for it later." Since you're used to listening to such voices, you do as you are told.

✔ After a while, you find that the very light weight you are bearing is not that light at all; in fact, it's kind of annoying.

✔ You go around asking people if they will help you take off the pack. They refuse, mostly because the weight you're carrying doesn't seem very important to them, who are so busy with so many important things. "We're too busy with so many important things," they say to you. "That's your weight, and if you ask us it doesn't seem that much to us. What're you? A sissy?"

✔ You understand now that your difficulties with the tiny fruit-cake on your back are making you look weak and small as it is. You are in danger of being defined as "the guy with the fruitcake problem." You are in despair.

✔ Finally, one dark and stormy night, you tear open your back-pack and eat every last crumb of the fruitcake. It's stale, but good. Best of all, it's gone.

✔ There is a flash of light and the voice is back. "Thanks for taking care of that stupid fruitcake," it says. "I get one every year and I never know what to do with it."

The Strong Enemy

My good friends, for the second time in our history,
a British Prime Minister has returned from Germany
bringing peace with honour. . . . I believe it is peace for
our time. Go home and get a nice, quiet sleep.
British prime minister Neville Chamberlain,
after signing a nonaggression pact with
Adolf Hitler in September 1938, almost a year
to the day before Hitler invaded Poland

At first consideration, it would seem that the strong enemy
presents an insurmountable problem. In fact, he offers the
greatest opportunity, for the following reason:

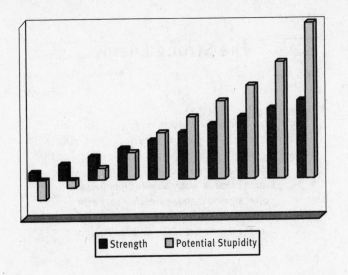

■ Strength ▢ Potential Stupidity

Yes, just as foolish, overconfident warriors can underestimate the supposedly weak enemy, it is equally ill-advised to be cowed by one who appears muscular and invincible. Nobody cannot be beaten, unless that is too many negatives for you, in which case I'll put it another way.

Everybody can be beaten. You just have to find the key. And as our chart demonstrates, the more indomitable a force gets, the more it thinks with its muscles instead of its head.

Strength makes people stupid. That's good news for you, because you're not stupid. Not as stupid as most really strong people are. That's because you can't rely on your strength, and they have to, because chances are they've abandoned everything else.

History is full of guys who started out pretty strong and very smart, and devolved into mighty powerhouses with bitsy-weeny little brain stems they didn't use very much.

LEADER	SMART AT START	STUPID LATER
Napoleon	Saved France	Invaded Russia
John Adams	Framed nation	Repressive Alien and Sedition Acts
Howard Hughes	Courageous airman	Total wacko
Pete Rose	Charlie Hustle	Bet on baseball
Michael Jackson	*Thriller*	"Jesus juice," i.e., wine and soda, offered to little boys
Jesse Ventura	Wrestler/actor	Governor of Minnesota
Bill Gates	Democratized computing	Anticompetitive thug
Jack Welch	Great CEO of GE	Randy dude with odd attitudes about company expenses
Howard Dean	Surprising front-runner	"I have a scream" speech

The fact is, human beings are not set up to be strong. We are an inherently weak species, prone to physical ailments, self-doubt, and inconstant bouts of cowardice and regret. The pressures of being strong are huge and the toll it takes on those who profess strength—and even some who possess the real thing—are your assets. You can manipulate that strength to your benefit, and, when necessary, trip up the muscle-bound hulk with a single line of twine.

STRONG ENEMY TACTICS

✔ The Japanese army is waiting on the outskirts of Tokyo for Godzilla to arrive. Then, there he is! Godzilla!

✔ The really stupid generals send a bunch of doomed idiots to attack Godzilla directly. They all get toasted by his fiery breath, their tiny toy jeeps melted into plastic blobs.

✔ The smarter scientist types hang back on the mountainside in their bunker, watching as the big lizard comes over the hills from the ocean and, squeaking and roaring, descends on the city.

✔ The good thing for Tokyo is that Godzilla is very large, yes, and very powerful, too, so strong that in the end he is able to destroy both Mothra and Megalon, among many others. At beating other monsters, he is a whiz.

✔ But while Godzilla is large and strong, he is not very smart. In movie after movie, he gets all tied up in electrical wires, which renders him so enraged, honking and squealing, that the smart warriors can attack him when he is at his worst.

✔ Bested again, sadder but still not much wiser in that mysterious limbic lump he calls a brain, Godzilla, tweeting and wheezing, sadly goes back into the ocean until mysterious factors cause him to return in the next sequel.

The Enemy You Hate

> People may hate each other. But when they are in
> the same boat crossing a river, they will row
> together very nicely.
> **Sun Tzu**

> But hatred is a much more delightful passion and never
> cloys; it will make us all happy for the rest of our lives.
> **Lord Byron**

The pains of war are many. The joys of war are few, at least while it is in full cry.

Perhaps the greatest ecstasy you are likely to experience in your career as a warrior is the soul-pleasing thrill of going to battle against an adversary you actually loathe.

Several things are true of this most deep, rich, and crucial test of your warrior spirit.

Most important is the fact that you have all the time in the world. For while love fades as doth the morning dew at times, a good hatred goes on forever, if you care for it and nurse it gently as a dedicated gardener tends his prize petunias.

It is here, in this case, that all the wealth of knowledge, preparation, dreaming, and lethal planning can be brought to bear, because a good hate—just like a good love—is not something to be wasted in rash action. You want to savor your hatred. Taste it. Imagine what it will be like to expiate all over the place when the time is right.

Ask yourself:

What is your adversary like? What does he enjoy? What does he fear? How long can you take to kill him in little cuts that hurt but do not incapacitate him for quite some time? What will injure him the most, but leave him conscious, so that he may know why this was done to him, and by whom?

What steps must you take to defend yourself over time, so that while you are in the midst of preparations or sneaking up from the rear, he or she does not surprise you with a gambit of his or her own?

What balance of surprise and anticipatory fear would you like to inflict upon him?

How long would you like him to suffer? Is your optimal ending to this saga his death, his humiliation, or a lingering life of misery to which you can be witness?

HATED ENEMY TACTICS

✔ Some enchanted evening, you will see a stranger across a crowded room, perhaps. It is clear from the very first moment that this is something that will last forever.

✔ Perhaps he or she hurts you first. You do nothing immediately about it. You're thinking. What is there about this person that keeps you up at night, festering?

✔ You strike back in some little way, and score some points. He or she is more careful around you after this. In corporate body language, you are circling each other.

✔ And then . . . you engage. It's public now. People know that you two are in it for real. You both gain in respect and fear, because a genuine hatred is awesome to those who look on.

✔ Time passes. There is no magic bullet you can put in the enemy. This is for real. It's not going away.

✔ You're going to need to move to the next level, one in which positioning and aggressive action are a daily way of life.

Part Six

Positioning

Don't be a naughty baby, come to papa,
come to papa, do . . . my sweet embraceable you.
Ira Gershwin

Grokking Your Corporate Tree

Which of the two sovereigns is imbued with Tao? Which
of the two generals has most ability? With whom lie the
advantages derived from heaven and earth?
On which side is discipline most rigorously enforced?
Which army is stronger? On which side are officers and
men more highly trained? In which army is there the
greater constancy both in reward and punishment?
Sun Tzu

Ask a stupid question, you get a stupid answer.
My grandmother

Sun Tzu spends a lot of time rooting around for good generals. People who wait for good generals to conduct battles
with them are about as lucky as poker players who wait for good
cards before they start betting.

You are not your boss, and his or her fate is not yours. While
he is preparing for your death, you may be excused for working
to implement a future of your own and, if necessary, plot for
his. I know that sounds cold, but loyalty to authority in wartime—at work, in any event—is a simple calculation for those
who do not cherish the idea of being a chump.

Loyalty: They Get What They Deserve

Loyalty (in%)

■ Their Loyalty to You ☐ Your Loyalty to Them

To do this, you're going to need to understand your own organization even more than that of your enemy, for the first enemies you will need to conquer will be the guys on your own side. Okay, they're not really enemies per se, but even though you drink with them, plan with them, hang with them, they are not really your friends, because they labor under the tragic delusion that their fate is just as important as yours. It's not.

If you're going to be a warrior, and not a soldier in somebody else's army, you're going to have to get used to this idea:

Relative Importance In Wartime

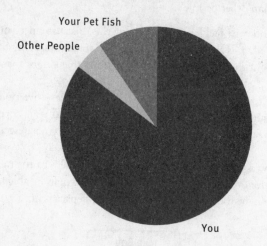

That's right. You are more important than anybody else. That's the first thing to get your mind around when you're getting positioned for battle.

The primacy of you bears with it certain implications:

1. You must live.

2. If others must die so you may live, so be it.

3. People who are far away when bombs go off are often around later, whereas those who are near the blast sometimes don't make it out; it is therefore probably a good idea to stay away from the worst of the fighting if you can help it.

4. You can do this only if you have the power to delegate some of the battle to others, or arrange the actual fisticuffs

in such a way that your nose is less likely to be punched than other people's.

5. You can't feel bad about any of this, because since your welfare is the primary concern you are always doing the right thing if you are doing the thing that's right for you.

In order to set up your chessboard with these five points as your guiding principle, you need to understand your corporate organization so that it can be manipulated to your best advantage.

Now again, warrior, we are not referring here to the rational, objective organization chart that someone would be able to reference if he looted the files of your HR department:

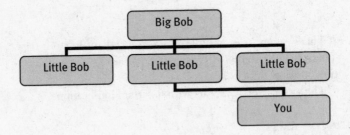

Of course you need to study the chart above and grok all its intense implications, no doubt about it. Obviously, yours is more complex and subtle than the one I've provided. And you absolutely do need to think about how it's structured and what its concrete forms and relations mean to you.

So look at it, daily, and don't look away. Spend the rest of your life looking, looking. And thinking, thinking. Who would fight with you? Watch your back? Kill you in a heartbeat?

And once you've looked and thought and all that, which is both necessary and good, and fully comprehended who's who,

who plays what, and what pieces can be bumped into one another to your advantage, it's time to move to this model:

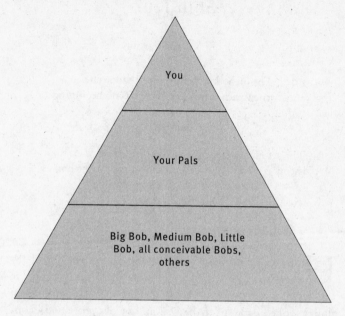

You

Your Pals

Big Bob, Medium Bob, Little Bob, all conceivable Bobs, others

And let me tell you something—if that's not the way you plan to move forward from here on in, you're wasting your time in this warrior business. Be something else in your workaday world. There are lots of slots for people who are too sensitive, thoughtful, and nonviolent and insufficiently enamored of their own destiny to be warriors. You can be one of those.

It's a living, for sure.

The rest of you? Let's start arranging all moving parts so that our chances of success are maximized.

Shih Tzu?

The orthodox and the unorthodox circle
and renew each other, as a circle has no beginning
and no end.
Sun Tzu

The art of war is simple enough. Find out where your
enemy is. Get at him as soon as you can. Strike him as
hard as you can, and keep moving.
Ulysses S. Grant

Ulysses S. Grant was a terrible politician, maybe one of the
worse presidents the United States has ever enjoyed. He
was also a great general. At the apex of the Civil War, when
things looked darkest for the Union, Lincoln promoted Grant
to run the Union armies. Critics were dubious, informing the
president of Grant's many shortcomings, including the fact that
he drank. "Find out what he's drinking," Lincoln replied, "so I
can give it to the rest of my generals."

Drink may have been the factor that gave Grant his edge. Shih
is that edge—the approach to your physical positioning that
makes it possible for us to forget worrying about issues like
strength and aggressiveness, and focus on the where, the when, the
how of battle. It's very important. I'm sure everybody with a good
understanding of Shih is racking up huge career points, preparing
for everything conceivable before they get to the actual fighting.

Sun Tzu says:

The rush of water, to the point of tossing rocks about. This is Shih.

The strike of the hawk, at the killing snap. This is the node.

Therefore, one skilled at battle—His shih is steep. His node is short.

Shih is like drawing the crossbow. The node is pulling the trigger.

Get it? Of course you do. You've been spending your whole professional life doing it. Preparing. Making sure you're not out of position when important meetings and conflicts take place.

Face it. You're full of Shih.

During the last twenty years or so, there hasn't been a single day that I didn't spend at least part of it thinking about some aspect of Shih. Shih topics of importance to me now and in the past include:

1. Giving good phone

2. Taking excellent meeting

3. The Tao of lunch

4. Drinking on the job

5. Proper (and improper) sucking up

6. Office furniture as a power tool

7. The art of internal correspondence

8. Destabilizing adversaries without being detected

9. Expense accounts: what's up with them?

10. Life on the road and other big dangers

The deal is, if you spend your life up to your neck in all that Shih, you kind of lose the knack of handling the "killing snap," or "node," that the Master refers to. And all the Shih in the world doesn't mean a thing unless you can pull the ripcord when node time comes.

Take the idea of never attacking an enemy where he is the strongest, but searching for an opening where He is Not. It's an intriguing notion. It's sort of useful when you think about it. "To advance so that one cannot be resisted, charge against the empty," Tzu writes. "The skilled general forms others, but himself is without form."

I like this a lot, the idea of forming others but being without form yourself. How this applies to fighting people who are themselves nothing, in essence, but enormous muscles of aggression I will leave to you. Honestly, I have no idea.

I also like the whole notion of attacking where the other guy isn't. The problem with it, for me, is that a lot of the time after I've attacked where he isn't I'm left to stand around wondering where he is.

Getting in Formation

These are the kinds of terrain: accessible, entangling,
temporizing, narrow, steep, far and near. The superior
general knows the ground on which he must fight.
Sun Tzu

We are not retreating.
We are advancing in another direction.
General Douglas MacArthur

Now, it's important that we make a distinction between two
entities, both of which are crucial to your wartime effort
before it even begins:

1. Aggression

2. Stupidity

The aggressive warrior spends enough time on Shih to know
he's not running into the business end of a bayonet.

The stupid warrior ignores the Shih and ends up impaling
himself on his enemy's node. Ooh. That hurts.

One hundred fifty years ago or so, the very brave and aggressive British Army was fighting the Russians in what later became
known as the Valley of Death. That's a bad start right there.

So this well-armed, intelligent, and courageous force of British
soldiers rode directly into an ambush in an enclosed space where

they could be slaughtered pretty much at will. And so they were. All of them. The best thing you can say about what happened to them is that a very nice poem was written by Tennyson celebrating their stupidity, oops, I mean their heroism.

In business, which I suppose we should talk about eventually, stark and disheartening examples abound of guys who fought the right battle on the wrong turf.

My old chairman, for example, won a major battle against his lunk-headed then-adversary by accosting his boss—everybody's got one—on a golf course outside of Pittsburgh, and wresting agreement from the old man to buy a subsidiary he wanted. The then-adversary later went on to be my chairman's chairman, and decapitated him by divesting the subsidiary that had been so cleverly won. The terrain changed, and that changed everything.

There are, in fact, dozens and dozens of mergers, made over the last hundred years or more, that were based on assumptions about the business terrain that were excessively hopeful, lacking in information, or just plain deluded. Others, like the wedding of Daimler and Chrysler, judged the playing field correctly and resulted in a nice new company that makes better cars, as anyone who has driven a PT Cruiser recently will attest.

Such examples are the exception, however. Most mergers are wars of conquest undertaken for the wrong reasons and fought by one or both parties on terrain that later proves not to be what it first appeared.

It's hard to be too severe about this. It's easy to see the reality of any given terrain after the battle is over and the field is strewn with bodies.

Since you don't want to be one of those corpses rotting in the sun with big, ugly birds eating out your eyeballs, it may be wise, as you get in formation to march into battle, to ask yourself whether you are making hopeful or ill-informed assumptions about the terrain and how to play on it. In fact, let's be sissies for a minute and use Mr. Tzu's designations for a quick assessment. It's difficult to comprehend how to apply the Master's strategic suggestions in a real-world situation, but we'll try.

Accessible terrain: People come and people go with relative freedom. This is the normal terrain of everyday business. Sun Tzu says we should be aggressive and maintain the high ground, and suggests this is an advantageous venue for battle.

Okay, so like, what's the high ground? The concept has changed since Sun Tzu's day.

ASPECTS OF HIGH GROUND

Ancient Chinese Warlord	Benefit	Contemporary Warrior
Good altitude	See enemy coming	Good attitude, excellent e-mail, spies
Good place for fort	Hard to attack, easy to defend	Decent office space, nice furnishings
Safe for provisions	Easy to establish permanent presence	Unassailable expense account
Ease of attack/retreat	Kill others, remain safe, lose least amount of men/provisions	Good delegation skills, sufficient staff to sustain losses and defections

Ancient Chinese Warlord	Benefit	Contemporary Warrior
Intimidate enemy	Minimize chance of unwanted engagement	Good internal/ external profile

High terrain, if we are to understand it in any helpful way whatsoever, is about making sure you have superior information and power in ordinary situations, and using that advantage to set the time and circumstances of battle, retreat, and provisioning.

Entangling terrain: This is described in sissy terms as ground where it is easy to go, but hard to return. If the enemy is unprepared, you may reveal yourself and attack, Tsays Tzu, and there is a good possibility of Tzuccess. If, on the other hand, the enemy is prepared, you may emerge and not be victorious. Since the mere possibility of engagement without success immediately renders battle Tzummarily impossible, and since once involved in battle it will be difficult to escape or retreat, this terrain is considered not advantageous.

Look at it this way: Comcast decides that it's going to make a bid for Disney. It fields an offer that, it turns out, is widely perceived as way too low. But oops. Now it's out there—entangled.

That is, it's hangin' out there. How many times has that happened to you? You're called upon to make a number of decisions every day. Once you express yourself on the subject, you're there, you know? You can retreat in some cases, but in others backtracking may not be quite so easy. Is this a reason not to engage, because it's not frickin' accessible?

Well, to some extent, yes, even if you're not a complete Tzissy.

But those who simply decide that entangled terrain is useless for battle are likely to get a reputation for Japanese reticence in the face of any decision for which they could be held accountable.

Here's what it looks like:

Temporizing terrain: In this scenario, both sides emerge and look at each other. If his forces are obviously weaker than yours, you may attack, although what he's got hidden in the trees—or at the Petaluma office—may be of concern. This is stasis, and once again the Master says this is not an advantageous time to wrestle with the foe, and of course he is right as far as that goes, but come on. So it's not advantageous! Grow a pair, will ya?

I am now so annoyed with the whole concept of terrain that I just want to go out and mash somebody. So let's move on.

On Deception

All warfare is based on deception. When able to
attack, seem unable. When deploying forces, feign
inactivity, when we are near, convince the enemy you
are far; when far away that you are near. Hold out
bait to entice him. Feign disorder and crush him:
If he is angry, goad him.
Sun Tzu

Off with her head!
The Red Queen

Deception is good, as long as you don't end up believing
your own deception. And become imprisoned by it.

Let me tell you what I mean. When I was a young man, I determined that I didn't like to do dishes. I liked to eat off the dishes all
right, but when the meal was done, the task of cleaning them up
was one I had no desire to pursue. It wasn't that I liked to eat off
dirty dishes, either. I liked clean dishes as much as the next bour-
geois. I just didn't want to be the one who cleaned them.

This often created conflict between me and the person I was
living with. Every now and then, she would say, "Why don't
you do the dishes for a change?" And I would be hard-pressed
to figure out a rational reason for not doing so. "I don't want
to" didn't seem to cut it after a while, and this being after 1970
(in America), it wasn't automatically assumed that it was the
role of women in this world to clean up after men. Not only

was there no rational argument against that development, there was no safe one.

So I developed a strategy that I later extended to a variety of household chores and much of the obnoxious grown-up stuff of life. I simply made myself so incompetent at anything I didn't want to do that after a time no one asked me to do it anymore.

By the time I reached my late thirties, I was seldom called upon to clean dishes (including loading the dishwasher), balance checkbooks, vacuum carpets, pay bills at the end of the month, or shovel snow.

The problem with the deception was this: while I didn't need to do many dishes, I had also become a really evasive fellow, well practiced at the art of choosing what I could and could not say and do by how much it might benefit me at the time.

Here are the problems inherent in a deceptive modus operandi:

✔ Like I said, you become a deceptive person. Deceptive people have a lot harder time garnering and maintaining the loyalty of others, and for good reason—they're liars!

✔ You become the lies you tell, simply because it's much easier to do that than to keep track of what's true and what isn't. I started out cleverly being deceptive about my ability to do the things I mentioned. Now I really stink at them.

✔ You will be caught. Let me repeat that. You will be caught. They will then stop trusting you. The first people to do this will not be your enemies, who you are quite successfully fooling à la Sun Tzu, but your friends and loved ones.

✔ You will then hate yourself, kind of, even in the midst of the ongoing orgy of self-love that motors your business

[153]

career. Believe it or not, that contempt for yourself will make you a far less effective warrior.

✔ You will eventually find that you are spending a lot more time crafting deceptions than killing other people. That's a waste of your time and talent, you know?

✔ When it comes to leading other people to war, or even keeping them from making you walk the plank when things get rough, you must remember to be deceptive with enemies and NOT be deceptive with friends. The problem is, I don't think that can be done. People who get good at being deceptive lose the ability to be good at being straight.

✔ And finally, when you actually win the war and must govern the territory you have conquered, you will be a weaselly loser who doesn't know what to do with the toy now that he has won it.

People in business love this part of Sun Tzu's doctrine, and that's because too many have been taught to be weasels instead of eagles.

Me? I want to walk up to a guy and know that if I push him hard enough he's going to fall down and kick his wing tips in the dirt and cry for his mommy. And you don't get that by all the fancy tap dancing in the Tao of deception.

Ultimately, lies are a defense. Truth is the best offensive weapon.

Part Seven

War

Banish omens and superstitious doubts and
even death itself loses its fearsome aspect.
Sun Tzu

The gods must be crazy.
African proverb

Transforming with the Enemy

Watch me pull a rabbit out of a hat.
Nothing up my sleeve . . . presto! Oops. Wrong hat.
Bullwinkle T. Moose

One of the qualities of a successful businessperson—this is most true of those who have attained executive status—is a certain crazy rigidity of character. Think about it. You've gotten to a certain point in your career by playing the game a certain way. You're not inclined to change that game now.

This rigidity of personality results in the phenomenon, obvious in people with reservoirs of power, of *always being 100 percent themselves, no matter how deplorable a thing that might be.* The world changes around such people; they do not change for it.

There are pluses and minuses to the rigid, authoritarian personality:

UPSIDE	DOWNSIDE
Sticks to guns	Never admits mistakes
Believes in self	. . . even when shouldn't
Decisive	Impulsive
Bold	Foolhardy

UPSIDE	DOWNSIDE
Won't take "no" for answer	Doesn't listen
Tough	Vicious
Takes responsibility	Thinks all ideas are his own
Visionary	Delusional

Two things suggest themselves in this lineup of assets and liabilities:

1. Such people need rigorous management by their subordinates if they are not to shoot themselves in the foot, quite literally. This control of the runaway rigid type is the job not of officers superior to them—who generally rely on their insanity—but of us who serve them. Every one of the downside traits offers opportunities for the savvy, bold warrior to assist (i.e., manipulate) his or her Master.

   If they are stubborn, for instance, you may keep them informed of things that should move them off the dime. When they finally, grudgingly, move to a better position, they will remember, for a while, how hard it was to do what you have done, and possibly even appreciate it.

   If they are delusional, you may act as a reality check, or not, as you see fit.

   Remember—all executive weakness and bizarreness represent not problems but chances to manage the forces that are supposed to be managing you.

2. Unless some moderation is effected in the general's rigidity (or your own, if you are the general), there's going to be

trouble in your war effort. Sun Tzu, always at his best when discussing the strategic and tactical side of things, states repeatedly, in his own difficult and impenetrable way, the need for the warrior to *improvise*, and, more important, to alternate orthodox with unorthodox, the expected with the unexpected.

Such behavior is exactly what your basic stick-up-the-butt warrior has trouble with. If that is you, you must think, as you pursue the active side of the war you are now undertaking, how you can modulate your own personality in order to transform with the enemy as he or she changes, moves around, gets stronger or weaker, more reticent or more aggressive.

Transformation is the opposite of rigidity. You can begin to acquire this capability by pursuing the following steps every day:

- ✔ Listen to what other people have to say for at least five minutes per twenty-four hours, even if what they're saying is boring to you, stupid, completely wrongheaded, obnoxious, and worthy of scorn. Listen. And as you listen, allow the other person's words to seep into you and change you just a little bit. Just the act of listening, probably somewhat foreign to you, will itself change you slightly, if you let it.

- ✔ Contemplate your enemy and what he is up to. Think the following thought: "What would I do if I weren't completely sure that I was doing the right thing all the time? Would I change my plans or methods?" Even if it just means altering the color of your socks for a day, do that. Start changing little things about yourself in direct response to things you have noticed in your foe. If you are used to waking up early and he doesn't get active until noon, try lazing about over breakfast and kicking in when he does. If he likes to leak stuff to the media and you're dead opposed to that, consider trying a little of his own medicine on him.

✔Change your eating habits slowly not to eat any one thing, but to surprise yourself with what you are putting into your body. If you are a strict fruit and yogurt woman, try some French toast on yourself one morning, with bacon. What you are trying to do is bend your character so it is less likely to travel only in well-established grooves. The world is a big place, with lots of options and many ways of doing things. You have to train yourself to see that and respond not only in expected but also unexpected ways.

✔Once a week, ask for a suggestion from somebody and do what he says, even if you find it difficult. See what happens.

✔Buy a hat. Not a baseball cap, everybody wears those and most people look as terrible as Michael Moore does in them. No, buy a fedora or a boater or a porkpie or a straw chapeau of some sort, and wear it on the weekends. You will feel different in your hat, after a while. And feeling different is what it's all about.

✔If you hate opera, go to one. If you hate football, attend a game. If you are tone deaf, take singing lessons. If you're married, take your spouse out to something odd. Go camping. Watch the sunrise. Dare to eat a peach.

Your enemy is presenting you with new options and challenges every day. If you respond in a wholly expected way each time, you will become predictable, and a predictable enemy is much easier to defeat than one who treats his adversaries to a surprise on a regular basis.

In short, there are things that should be expected in war and in business:

THINGS THAT SHOULD BE PREDICTABLE IN A LEADER

Force is met with force

Troops are paid on time

No crying

Generally consistent body weight

Generally consistent working hours

No singing except at public functions

No air guitar in the office

No expletives except under extreme fucking duress

Consistent costume consonant with corporate values

General expressions of respect for authority

...and things that should not.

THINGS THAT SHOULD NOT BE TOTALLY PREDICTABLE

Tactics of aggression

Tactics of retaliation

Eating and drinking habits

Mood

Preparations for battle

Acts of generosity

Moments of public rumination

When he or she will yell

This mix of predictable and unpredictable will become an important part of the warrior you will be. To reach this goal, you will need to tune in to your friends and enemies alike, and focus on the physical, emotional, financial, and intellectual environment in which you will run your war. And transform yourself accordingly. Sound tough? Well, it shouldn't be. Not if you put your face up to the elements, let out a gigantic roar, and embrace the chaos that is human conflict.

This is War, not a stroll in the park! It's what you came here for—simultaneously the highest and lowest expression of the animal we are and the civilization in which we live and die. Bring it on!

War by the Numbers

> He had killed and put to earth so many that
> his sword broke in two. At length he thought
> to himself that that was enough massacring and
> killing for one day, and that the rest should be
> allowed to escape in order to spread the news.
> **François Rabelais,**
> **Gargantua**

1. Clarify your goals and figure out how you plan to attain them, assuming that the preservation of enemy life is not an issue, at least at first.

2. What is it you want? Territory? The death of thousands? Gold? Dream big. There is no point in going to war for insubstantial or silly aims.

3. Here are some goals that were established in famous wars you may or may not have heard of:

WAR	GOAL
Trojan War	Destroy Troy/Hook up with Helen
U.S. Civil War	Secede from/Save Union
War of Spanish Succession	Spanish succession

WAR	GOAL
Hundred Years' War	Nobody knows
Diller vs. Redstone	Paramount

4. Declare war: It's best to do this immediately as you launch your first major offensive. War is generally begun by a simultaneous act and declaration. They go together. Both show that you mean business. So think about what your first shot is going to be.

5. Now seize the offensive: Both enemies and friends have been informed that the horrors and exhilarations of war are upon them, so it's time for everybody to get energized and excited. This is the time, before too much blood has been shed and everybody has forgotten what the whole thing was supposed to be about, when the greatest gains can be made by an aggressor.

6. A word about that. If you have to choose between the two roles—aggressor or defender—it's way better to be the former. Aggressors can win. Defenders' best hope is to not lose. You can see the difference. Strike early each day, and strike often. The war is to the swift and the mean.

7. Accumulate allies: Once you have demonstrated aggression and the willingness to hurt other people, you will begin to attract people who want to join with you for their own benefit. These are called allies. They're not as good as friends on the one hand or subordinates willing to die for you on the other, but they're worth something.

8. Your pool of allies is made up of several groups:

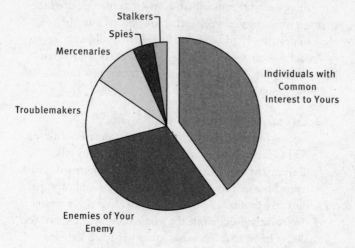

Stalkers

Spies

Mercenaries

Troublemakers

Individuals with Common Interest to Yours

Enemies of Your Enemy

9. A word about spies: Aside from consultants, they are the most obvious expression of a diseased social environment. In many cases, in fact, the spy is a consultant.

10. Spies are good for the getting of data and the planting of false information into the enemy camp. The assumption you should make during wartime is that spies are always working for both sides of the conflict and, in the end, themselves. This makes them perhaps the most consistent and trustworthy entities with which you, as a leader and warrior, are likely to deal. You can always depend on a spy to do what spies do, whereas friends, enemies, and subordinates can sometimes do unexpected things. And the unexpected, in a war, is to be avoided at almost any cost.

11. Seize the media: You'd be amazed to truly grasp how important propaganda is to your purpose. Think about

the way Kim Jong Il, the demented, egomaniacal martinet who runs North Korea, has manipulated the gigantic cultural images that are poured into the understimulated brains of his worried subjects. Streets and flowers are named after him. Operas are written about him. If they had more electricity, just think what they could do.

12. Let's take a minute about your PR effort.

Jesus himself had the four apostles, plus, at a later date, Mel Gibson. Samuel Johnson, a fat, witty guy who illuminated the eighteenth century, had a talented scribe named Boswell who followed him around and captured his every fatuity. Trump has himself. Every war master controls the story while the whole thing is going on. You always know that a side has lost a war when they lose control of the press.

The thing you need to know about the press, if you have any dealings with the nice, smart people who do that grubby job, is that the thing they want most is a story. If there is no story, still they want a story. Stories they like:

✔ Fiduciary irresponsibility

✔ Sex stuff

✔ Cultural dissonance

✔ Celebrity gossip/factoids

The most important thing for them, without fail, is the need to feed the beast every day. Think about it. They have a hundred pages of content to frame around their advertising each time they show up at work. Imagine that.

It's tough. So if you give them a story, no matter how gooshy, fractile, or brain damaged, they will listen. This is terrific for you in your war, because if you are aggressive in this sphere as you are on the battlefield, you will define the way the war is perceived, and that, my friends, is the whole deal.

13. Now start killing people. Didn't you know that was what this was all about?

14. It's always surprising to me that people are grossed out or shocked that war involves the killing of people. You're lucky. You're in business, not in the actual business of war. War—real War—truly sucks. Even one human life is precious. And what have millions been lost pursuing? What stupidity? And always in the name of right and justice?

15. But you? You're lucky. You're conducting a sissy war, because nobody is going to die, not really. And you're at a huge advantage because, thanks to me, you are not a total goddamned sissy.

16. People at war have been required to justify an enormous Tzunami of horrible things they have done to their adversaries. The business universe pales by comparison.

17. About killing people: It's hard in the beginning and then, if you are a decent person, it gets very slowly easier until it seems like business to you. If you are not a decent person, so much the better for you. This makes you valuable, up to a point. Ultimately, however, people will be disgusted with you, so be careful displaying the fact that you have no conscience about these things. You may think it's a business asset. It's not.

18. You may ask, "Who am I supposed to kill?" This should be obvious to you, once you think about it. If it's not, you're not truly engaged in battle. What's the matter with you? Shape up!

19. Now let's look at a couple of ways you can hack through other people on your way to success:

   a. Humiliation: This is a more pointed and vicious weapon than you might guess. It's relatively easy to repair one's position after having been screamed at. Far more difficult is to stand tall when the ground under one's feet is infested with worms.

   Remember that business warfare is rarely a Sun Tzu–style blitzkrieg that is over before the general's coffee gets cold. It's more the other Chinese contribution to world culture: the water torture. There is no more terrible thing to witness than two enemies locked in an endless death grip while one humiliates the other until that other can take it no longer. I've seen grown men and women sustain continued small, painful injury to their soft tissue over a period of months and months and then, eventually, unable to take any more, simply depart, leaving severance and options on the table worth quite a bit of green.

   Corporate behavior is circumscribed. How a person is allowed to react to torture depends on one's rank, physical equipment, and the power of those above and below in their reporting structure. A vendor, for example, may *never* yell at a purchasing officer, no matter how insulting or damaging he might be. A campaign of humiliation, conducted correctly, will succeed in complete and total *evisceration* of the enemy with virtually no danger to the aggressor.

b. Decapitation: At times, however, we don't have the leisure to enjoy each individual death or dismemberment. Business must be done. The battle must be concluded and other aspects of the war pursued. That's when we must smite our adversary's head from his shoulders with one masterful stroke.

   The removal of the other fellow's head is usually pretty easy, since it is rarely securely attached to his shoulders these days.

   Be careful. Some executives have been known to do extensive damage to others *after* they have lost their heads. Make sure both the head and the body are rendered inert before you move along to the next foe.

c. Defenestration: This may be defined as the action of hurling another person out of the window. It may be taken after humiliation of the enemy, when he or she is weak and almost wants to be hurled, or to the body of an antagonist whose head has long since ceased to work.

20. You're getting somewhere. Slicing through the small fry, one eventually reaches larger fish, and as all true mobsters know, the fish stinks from the head. Cut off the head, the fins will die. That's if you're interested in dead fins. There may be other parts of the fish that you want to kill. A fish's liver, for instance, is disgusting, particularly if it has been drinking.

21. Sometimes, however, the leadership of your enemy may be boned and planked, and yet the war goes on. Now it becomes a battle for the hearts and minds of the people. At this point, once again your PR effort becomes ever more important. Look for powerful, high-profile acolytes to gain you credibility. Following are some famous campaigns and the endorsements that gave them the impetus they needed to get over the top.

Product	Spokesperson
The British Empire	Rudyard Kipling
Alfred Dreyfus	Emile Zola
Benito Mussolini	Ezra Pound
Westinghouse refrigerator	Betty Furness
Wella Balsam shampoo	Farrah Fawcett
Habitat for Humanity	Jimmy Carter
Jell-O	Bill Cosby
Pepsi	Britney Spears
Get More (T-Mobile/ Michael Douglas)	Catherine Zeta-Jones

22. Now it's time to open up other fronts for conflict. But you have to be careful. A great new front can bring in new soldiers, new revenue streams, new meat for your

grill. It can also overextend you and make your best-laid plans gang a-gley, as Robert Burns said. In English? Go too far and you'll screw yourself up. But stay put and you're not really conquering anything, are you.

23. New fronts: Back in the glory days of the Third Reich, Hitler was doing fine until he made the mistake of opening up an eastern front against Russia. After that, it was only a matter of time before Germany, with its resources spread thin over the entirety of Europe, began its slow fall into failure and escape to sunny South America.

   Here are some other fronts that have been opened by warriors through the years, for better and in some cases for way, way worse. You, of course, will do better than they.

WARRIOR	ORGANIZATION	NEW FRONT
Various Caesars	Rome	Russell Crowe
Ben (Bugsy) Siegel	Mafia	Las Vegas
Akio Morita	Sony	Lew Wasserman
Sam Walton	Wal-Mart	Semiautomatic weapons
Bud Selig	Baseball	Juiced-up players
Roberto Guizueta	Coke	Water
P. Diddy	Bad Boy	Oversized clothing

24. The war is now waging on a number of fronts. You have successes and failures every day. You are patient, because you know that life is war and that there will never be an end to the latter until you're pretty much done with the former.

25. So fight on, warrior! And good luck!

26. Fear not!

27. Stay in touch!

Cowardice and Bravery

Cowardice is the mother of bravery.
Sun Tzu

Cowardice shuts the eyes of the
mind and chills the heart.
Ralph Waldo Emerson

Sun Tzu believed that it was bad form to require courage from little people. He said that you should simply pour people into the right Shih and the rest would take care of itself, sort of. Once again, this does not conform to any reality that I've experienced, although there is truth in it. If you back people up against a wall, they will fight for their lives with great spirit, no courage required.

The truth is that if you go into a battle situation knowing that you've got the goods to cream the other guy from the outset, well, that's a good feeling. I'm sure we all wish that was always so, and great strategists tend to create these kinds of advantageous situations for themselves. You can too, if you possess:

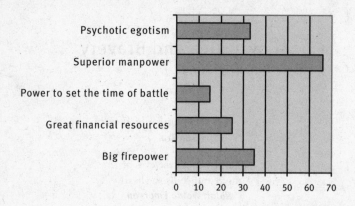

Such assets, however, are relatively rare. Most of the time, we function with far less:

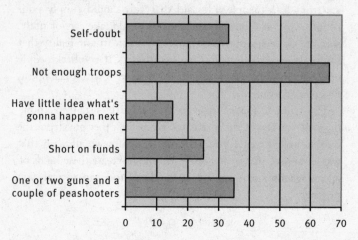

How much more courageous are we, then, we who wrestle with the beast each and every day in spite of our inTzufficiencies? Make no mistake, warrior. You will need plenty of courage to sleep each night a sweet, dreamless, restful slumber that recharges you for the challenges of the morrow, to wake each morning with the requisite fire in your belly, to soldier on through mire and blood battle after battle.

This cannot be done without tremendous bravery, because the natural condition of humanity is careful, intelligent cowardice. This is why we continue to evolve as a species and the trilobite and allosaurus did not. We're smart. We avoid potentially dangerous situations. In order to summon courage in the face of almost certain injury and aggravation, we need to feel loyalty for and from our organization and affection for our commanding officer, and, yes, we need to have a little bit of fun.

Part Eight

Whistle While You Work

Happiness is a warm gun.
John Lennon

Stupid Sun Tzu Stuff, Part XIV:
Only a Short War Is Worth Waging

No nation ever benefitted from a prolonged war.
Sun Tzu

I've been loving you too long to stop now.
Otis Redding

As for Sun Tzu's assertion that all wars must be short and to the point, it remains only to observe that just because a guy is a sissy doesn't mean he can't also be an optimist.

Some wars are brief. But you can't count on them to be.

In fact, for the most part, business wars are not fought in the short term. They are marathons that never end, not sprints with victory laps and champagne at the end of each merry conquest.

That's why it's important to drink the champagne whether you're winning or not.

The big sissy-boy is not all wrong. A long conflict does drain resources, costs a lot of money, and wears down the morale of the army. Of course, all of that is true. But all that means is that you, if you plan to hang in there and keep the battle raging, will need constant refreshment of your resources, tons of money all the time, and an army that feasts on conflict and is bored and restive when not in battle.

Think about the Orcs in *Lord of the Rings*. Can you imagine them doing anything but marching and fighting? Can you see them hanging around the bowling alley having a few beers on a Wednesday night? No. They're Orcs. They fight for the forces of evil. You're like that.

So, how do you keep your resources strong, yourself in funds, and morale so high you could sing about it?

By having fun every day. And being fun to have war with.

This sounds improbable, I know, but great business warriors spend more time having fun than they do planning their strategies and exercising on the open field. There is a direct relationship between how much fun a person has on the job every day and how ready he or she is to protect that way of life and, when possible, expand it.

Fun and Success: A Direct Correlation

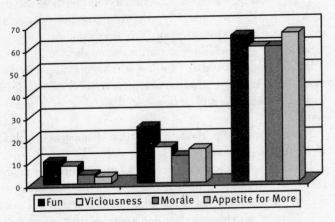

As you see, small fun creates even fewer of the attributes that make sustained warfare both palatable and possible—viciousness, good morale, and a pleasantly nagging appetite for more.

Of course, one person's idea of fun is another's idea of a hot poker in the eye. A list of great warriors makes this point very clearly.

WARRIOR	IDEA OF FUN
David	Bathsheba
Vlad the Impaler	Impaling
Henry V	Wassailing
Henry VIII	Eating mutton/beheading wives
Bob in the mailroom	Two beers
Mike Ditka	Two Levitra
Richard Branson	Ballooning
Your VP of Sales	Six martinis/passing out

See? Everybody's different, so everybody's idea of a good time is different. My friend Rafferty thinks it's fun to wander around the streets of foreign cities like Minneapolis at night, drinking himself into a coma. Many people I know actually mix business with golf, both of which would seem to be sufficiently aggravating pastimes in their own right. But there's no accounting for taste.

So have a blast at what you do. And if you're not, change your game. Nobody's going to declare world peace anytime soon, and until then you might as well knock yourself out.

Somebody's Gonna Suffer
(Not You.)

War is exhilarating. War elicits loyalty, solidarity.
War gives us purpose and drive. War was what I wanted.
War was who I was. The Music Warrior was about to
move. I gathered my forces. I gave my hyped-up speeches.
I set my sights on the competition and the first thing
I saw was James Taylor. Wouldn't it be wonderful to steal
JT from Warner? What a way to start the war!

Walter Yetnikoff,
former head of
CBS Records

That's the voice of the insane corporate warrior, the kind
who walks into a minefield 100 percent sure that the only
one who will not be blown up on this fine summer's day is himself. And so he's not. Such people lead charmed lives, and pull a
ton of folks under the bus before they have to go.

The beauty part of business warfare, unless your business is
importing cocaine from Colombia or covering up a nuclear fuel
spill in the Midwest, is that there is rarely any actual blood involved. Maybe that's why we can forgive Sun Tzu now and then
for being such a careful sissy-boy. His guys were playing with
live ammo, not cell phones and BlackBerrys.

There's no question, however, that violence is a bad, bad
thing, particularly for the people who get hurt by it. I hope

you've thought about that long and hard before you go plunging off to war willy-nilly without a care in the world.

If you did, and I'm sure you wouldn't lie to me about a thing like that, you have undoubtedly come to the conclusion that as long as somebody has to suffer from the war, you'd much rather that it be somebody other than you.

There is a hierarchy of suffering that all great generals, and even small ones like you, understand implicitly. Here are the people who, ideally, should suffer, in order of preference (yours):

* **The enemy:** Company A takes over Company B. "Apart, we were two great companies. Together, we are unstoppable!" says the chairman's memo when the entities merge. "Don't worry," says the Human Resources executive when all the nervous people in Company B ask him what's going to happen to deal with certain . . . redundancies, "we're looking for the best and the brightest and we don't care whether you're an A-person or a B-person. If you're excellent, you're part of the new team." Two weeks later, everybody from Company B loses their offices, their jobs, and their access to lunch. How come? Because the winner doesn't want to suffer. The loser suffers. Ergo, if you're suffering? You're a loser. Go out there and make other people suffer. Then you'll be a winner.

* **Your allies, friends, and soldiers:** Sometimes it is necessary for your own side to feel the sting of war. People die, even people close to you. Such is life. That's the way the cookie crumbles. Or the old ball bounces, if it does. So within this big hierarchy of suffering there is a smaller one that you should try to take into consideration moving forward:

➤ Guys you hate: Certainly, there are some within your own band who you could do without.

➤ Guys not in your part of the reporting structure: Okay, you feel bad because you saw the guy at the last corporate retreat on Sanibel Island, but really, your life will go on just fine without him, right?

➤ Consultants, spies, and ill-defined players: Every organization has a few of these, and they are almost always fungible. They are purportedly on your side, but could turn at any time and are not to be trusted anyhow. Tripping them into a vat of lava is almost doing them a favor.

➤ Guys in your reporting structure whose job you could assimilate into your own, for more money. War is perhaps one of the greatest opportunity engines there are, both in the real world and in business. Deaths create gaps in the infrastructure that could be filled by you. Don't miss any.

➤ Guys you like: Goes without saying, right? There are few enough of them, I'm betting. Try to make their suffering almost as important as your own.

➤ Your boss. A power vacuum above you could well suck you into the next solar system. Even if you loathe him or her, one destabilizes or harms one's boss at one's own peril. And if that's too many Ones for you, let's just say Don't Do It. It may, in some cases, be better for you to take a nonlethal bullet than for you to permit your boss to endure a crippling injury. Don't think I'm suggesting blind loyalty or altruism here. I'm not. I'm simply saying that a bad thing for the guy who stands between you and the abyss is bad for you as well.

* You. Obviously, your job is to stay alive and suffer as little as possible. You can't enjoy the war if you're suffering too much. A little, maybe, to give life on the edge some spice. But don't take more than a shaving cut if you can help it.

Some things to avoid in your ongoing effort to avoid personal pain and enjoy the clank and scream of warfare:

✔ Sleepless nights: The trick, at the height of the battle, is to go out in the evening and wear yourself ragged so that you sleep like a stone for at least five hours. Five hours should do it for any warrior, by the way. Then up and at 'em. You'll sleep when you're dead. Carousing with the troops and other generals builds morale and loyalty and makes the war go faster. Waking in the morning is rarely as much fun as you want it to be, though.

✔ Anxiety dementia . . . usually attacks at dawn. And it's hard not to be anxious if you're that type. I am. It doesn't matter that a lot of the time there's nothing really to be anxious about, in the sense that you're doing everything you can to win and probably should just chill out about the stuff that's not under your control. The problem is, you don't need a reason. That's why they call it "nonspecific anxiety." A word of warning: Drinking is not a long-term solution to the problem of anxiety. That's why you have to do it every day to renew its medicinal value.

✔ Depression: Too much drinking also leads to this malady. Also too little. The cure for depression, as any depressed person knows, is time, along with constant infusions of ego-massaging sucking up to you, provided by people who are dependent on you in the workplace and, if you can swing it, at home. Depression is very often based on free-floating anger directed at oneself—probably for good reason. The trick, if you are to keep your head above the goo, is to turn that anger away from yourself and inflict it on other people.

✔ Guilt: This approach, however, may lead to bad feelings about yourself afterward, particularly when you have done something to be ashamed of. If you haven't, by the way, you're probably not being a very effective warrior. There's nothing you can do about guilt except endure it until it fades. You will note that as you get more seasoned in the struggle you will be tortured by guilt more rarely, and the depth of the guilt-bucket will diminish until, when you're a real, grizzled pro, it's about the size of a walnut shell.

✔ Anhedonia: This is defined as the inability to enjoy yourself. It's a complete waste of time. Cut it out. God put you on this planet to revel in the beauty and majesty of existence.

Things You Can Do
While Waiting to Kill or Be Killed

And we'll have fun fun fun until
Daddy takes the T-Bird away.
The Beach Boys

My word. There are a million things that you can do to live your life while all around you are losing theirs. Here is just a rough breakout:

Drink: I don't want to make too much of the importance of alcohol in the conduct of business. Frankly, it's impossible to do so. I'm not saying that everybody should go out and get hammered all the time. That's just stupid. You always want to have some control over yourself and, more important, others, and you can't do that if you're being carried back to your hotel room, drooling and babbling, by your embarrassed subordinates.

But drink does several important things for you and the army you may or may not be fortunate enough to lead. First, as I've said, it builds teamwork and the false sense of personal intimacy upon which business unity is forged. It also plays a crucial role in inhibiting moral qualms and quashing feelings of guilt—until, possibly, the morning after.

The morning after, by the way, is a very delicate time of day for anyone who works for a living. It is the time in which you put on your face, squeeze your body into whatever garb best conceals its imperfections, decide what must be done—or not done—first, second, and third, or before the Furies descend on you. All of this is filtered through a soggy towel made of all the threads of your persona and how it truly feels before all the self-justification, rationalization, and stimulation sets in.

So, like I said. The early morning is tough. The goal is to get through it as quickly as possible and hit the first task of the day with energy and focus, blinding yourself to the bumpy realities that come through way too loud and clear before that third cup of coffee sinks in. You simply can't let the first hour of the day impinge on the rest of it. That's what unemployment is all about.

Play golf, PS2, Game Boy, etc: Games replicate the challenges of actual business—competition within a context that borders on the meaningless, feelings of superiority, inferiority, and loss, and in some cases, the need to rely on groups of people to get things done. Places to engage in these important activities include: golf courses, online, Vegas, in the office at night (if the game is poker), Monte Carlo, or, in many cases, the soccer, baseball, or football field of your kid's school. Many high-powered corporate soldiers enjoy coaching team sports involving their children, bringing the horrible values, ill-temper, and poor sportsmanship to a whole new generation that will one day take our place.

Travel: Going places to distract yourself is one of the prime opportunities of which businesspeople can legitimately avail themselves. There are many, many wonderful places in the world—and there's probably a pretty good reason you can get to every one of them before you are killed in battle and transported to Valhalla on your shield. Great cities for business include: New York, Chicago, Los Angeles, Seattle, San Francisco and its environs, including Napa and Sonoma, where much good strategic thinking can be done over several bottles of excellent Zinfandel, Boston (only in the spring or fall, though), Miami, New Orleans, and Las Vegas, if you're a complete degenerate. There's also Europe, which has many cities and nice hotels, and Asia, which is of such overweening strangeness that one visit there just might last you a lifetime.

Hotels are a terrific place to enjoy war, especially these days, where a room at the Four Seasons or Ritz is equipped with high-speed Internet, fax and phone, and room service up the proverbial wazoo. If the company allows you to get out and about, you're a bonehead if you and your wazoo don't seize the chance.

A word to the wise? Pack light. Nobody looks good hauling a big wheeliebag around after him. Could you see Napoleon humping around from Nantes to Marseilles with one of those things?

Torture people: You'd be surprised how much fun this can be for the bored or underexercised executive mind. There are few things more diverting, when one has nothing to do, than making junior officers and enlisted people run around in confusion and paranoia doing things that won't be remembered in about eight minutes. This is most often employed, in serious senior managers, as a means of weaning out those who aren't going to be able to take the heat when the kitchen gets warm later on. You may amuse yourself torturing subordinates in a variety of ways:

- ✔ Yelling at inappropriate times

- ✔ Assigning two people to the same chore

- ✔ Inviting, then disinviting people to prestigious events

- ✔ Giving the silent treatment to somebody you're used to speaking cordially with

- ✔ Dicking with their expenses

- ✔ Kicking back work that's perfectly fine with extremely vague criticisms that can't be understood or acted upon

- ✔ Putting a mouse on their chair (or other "funny" practical jokes)

- ✔ Lot of other stuff—use your imagination.

Have sex: Hotels are also excellent places for this purpose, as is the comfort of your own home, or somebody else's. There's really no bad place for it if you have the right person in mind. I'm not going to give you any advice here, because I'm sure you're doing fine anyhow. Suffice it to say that sex is probably the most diverting thing you can do to get your mind off war.

Better still, perhaps, is the love of family and companionship of nonbusiness friends with whom you can surround yourself to insulate your life from the indignities of harsh existence. Sadly, few really successful warriors have a whole lot of this kind of stuff. Probably just a coincidence.

Eat: Is there anything better than a big sausage submarine when you really want one? A gigantic steak? A baked potato with sour cream and synthetic bacon? A slab of fried fish and crispy hot freedom fries? Perhaps a peanut butter and jelly sandwich on Wonder Bread with a big old glass of cold milk? Yum yum yum! War seems a million miles away, don't it?

Buy cool stuff: You work hard for your money. One day, you may die for it. Hopefully, you'll cram your life with a lot of stupid effluvia that is just as much fun to buy as it is to own. Money can't buy happiness? Maybe not. But it can buy a $300,000, 543-horsepower Maybach 62.

Do business: Oh yeah. Let's remember that there's a whole lot of stuff you can do every day that has absolutely *nothing* to do with war at all. Let's see . . . there's that thing you were thinking about yesterday that you might like to do next year . . . why not work at that? What was it again?

Look out the window: There's an amazing amount of stuff going on in the street. People walk here and there. Cars go by. The little balloon vendor whistles far and wee. That kind of thing.

While doing this, you might have a few thoughts. Treasure these. If you take care of them and regard them closely, save them for a rainy day, you may find you have others. Pretty soon you'll be thinking. That can't be bad.

Part Nine

Booty Call

The victor belongs to the spoils.
F. Scott Fitzgerald

The Taste of Victory
(Hint: It Tastes Like Cheese)

A lot of counting rods is better than a few—and how
much better than none!
Sun Tzu

But purely military power,
even in its greatest dimensions of superiority,
can produce only short-term successes.
George Kennan

Like cheese, victory has many textures and flavors. And the
more you eat, the more discerning you become about them.

Cheddar, for example, is hard and tangy, like when Sandy
Weill succeeded in ousting John Reed in a very public brawl
over who would run the great big Citi.

A guy like Donald Trump has got to have a big, hearty cheese,
a little smelly, a little sweet, that goes great with ham. Swiss,
maybe. It's got holes in it.

Limburger is soft and nutty and really stinky, like Florida in
2000.

Visualize your own cheese. Imagine yourself eating it with a
slice of rugged brown bread, or perhaps a nice, thick cracker,
like Ted Turner.

Imagining your own triumph, tasting it before it is actually in
your hands, is a key part of winning, of being a winner.

Real warriors go to sleep at night with visions of cheese in their fat little heads. They don't wait until it happens to tally up their counting rods, whatever the heck those are.

They taste it in their sleep, then wake up hungry. And eventually, if you taste it, it will come.

Types of Booty

When an opening appears, move fast. Go straight
for the things he loves.
Sun Tzu

In war there is no prize for the runner-up.
General Omar Bradley

Good things come in all shapes and sizes, but in a business
war you enjoy some very specific payouts for all the conflict and suffering. Some are so valuable you should go for them
immediately to make sure that one of your own people doesn't
snatch them up for him- or herself. You didn't put up with all
this Shih to come away with a couple of ribbons and a pat on
the back from the guy who is suddenly in a better office than
yours.

Booty does not fall into your lap. You have to go and get it. In
some cases, ironically, you may have to fight for it after the war
is over. And remember, just because the president is on the deck
of the aircraft carrier with his thumb up in the air doesn't mean
the conflict has ceased. Now more than ever, the race is to the
strong and swift.

Go for **power** first. A long time ago, I was in a serious war for
control of a new, merged entity. Everything was in play for
about six months. Nobody knew who was going to run what
function. There were consultants around. The parent corporation was seeding all departments with bullet-headed screws.

There were vacuums everywhere you looked, like in a fine hotel first thing in the morning.

As the smoke and dust were clearing, I sought out the head of the culture that I thought was going to prevail, and asked him for the job I wanted. In order to make the point that he could do it if he wanted to, he did it. Then he had it announced to the press without running the contents of the release by his senior management. It was a ballsy thing to do. I was the tool, but a happy, singing tool.

Now, I could have been polite and waited for the system to work out the most equitable solution to the booty issue, but you know what? I'd done that before and ended up with the third office down the hall from the corner. I figured why not.

When the power arrives, don't forget to go for the **position**. Too many people are chumps in this regard. They figure, okay, I have the job, the responsibilities, what do I want with a big pompous title and all the trappings and Tinkertoys? Believe me, you want all that.

Think: There is a new, postwar government forming. Titles are more important in that environment than any other. People are generally ill-defined to each other and rely on the exterior branding to place strange faces in their proper power context.

If you are a vice president, you will be viewed as a certain level of player. If you are not, even if your duties far exceed those of the vice president, you will not be invited to vice-presidential events, and pretty soon you will be thought of as an excellent worker but not particularly management caliber. This, of course, is horse*shih*.

After **power** and **position**, you must accumulate the **tasks** that confer a different-colored sash. Look about you. Good tasks are floating about like paper money in one of those quiz show air tunnels where contestants get to keep all they can grab in fifteen seconds. Possible tasks you should keep an eye out for:

✔ Reorganization of any department whatsoever.

✔ Working in any way on any corporate utterance—this would include speeches, interviews, stockholder communications, TV or radio appearances, roasts, toasts.

✔ Budgeting any aspect of any function, preferably not your own, but if your own is being done, it's better to be in the driver's seat than be dragged along in the caboose while the generals are up in the club car.

✔ Organizing, planning, or attending any form of retreat or team-building exercise (or clandestine panty raid), for the most evident reasons in the world. A man or woman you get drunk with is 62 percent less likely to fire you in the next six months than one who has remained sober in your presence, and you in his.

Other prime chunks of booty one can go for include: **office space,** which will be available with all the "restructuring" and "consolidation of human resources" and "decruitment" going on after the first cease-fire is called.

In this regard, I know I don't have to tell you that there are two considerations in the evaluation of any office: volume of space contained within and positioning on the floor. That is, size and location. Corners are almost always best, for reasons that probably stretch back to the day when the first sentient cave-person chose a hole in the mountainside that seemed better to him or her than any other. Go for a big statement in your office.

Beyond that, there is, of course, **money** and **perks** and perhaps even **a new reporting relationship** for you with a brand-new powerful boss who has crushed yours in the fisticuff festival, all of which may be counted as the spoils of war.

But the most wonderful prize of all is **people**. In the process of winning, you will have the opportunity to add loyal troops who can live and die for you later.

Be careful, by the way, of worms and spies who have outlived their function and usefulness in the new world order. Guys who once had force and influence and now have less are very, very dangerous. They are often like those dye packets banks put in bags of stolen cash which, after a set period of time, explode and muck up everything and everybody in their vicinity.

Get rid of them.

Writing the Story

WAR IS PEACE.
FREEDOM IS SLAVERY.
IGNORANCE IS STRENGTH.

The Three Slogans of the Party
George Orwell,
Nineteen Eighty-Four

As the philosopher Walter Benjamin noted, and has been widely repeated without attribution since then—history is written by the winners. You now have the opportunity to create how people in the near and distant future perceive what you have done and what you have yet to do.

There are several venues for the construction of a workable story that will later function as history. They include:

- Newspapers, trade and consumer magazines, cable news programs that serve as conduits for uninterpreted messages of all kinds.

- Advertising, which is costly, but has enormous credibility in a consumer culture where ideas are as much of a product as sneakers.

- Internal newsletters, through which the Party can educate the masses.

Inclusion in books, which in the end stick around longer than any other medium, for better or worse.

Word of mouth: This will be the conduit for most of the tales celebrating your heroic legacy. That's okay. Beowulf. Genghis Khan. Howard Hughes. These are warriors whose mystery and greatness transcend mechanical marketing hype and enter the reality of oral history. You can do that too, on a smaller scale. My company and yours have figures shrouded in mist, some of them contemporary, some of them of the recent past, others who bestrode the earth in the days when the enterprise was just an idea in the head of some guy who couldn't get ahead doing anything else.

Each major war in the history of the human race was fought with two basic stories: the story of the winner and the story of the loser. Let's look at the record.

War	Winner's View	Loser's View	History's View
Trojan	Heroic, clever Greeks triumph over stupid, credulous Trojans	Sleazy, lying cheaters sneak into town and steal queen for lascivious purposes	Same as winner's

War	Winner's View	Loser's View	History's View
American Revolution	Feisty, freedom-loving colonists triumph over oppressive rule of the British Empire	Ungrateful, violent, disloyal traitors rebel against the eminently legal rule	Same as winner's
Napoleonic	Nutty, short, maniacal, tyrannical dictator is defeated, saving Europe	The sclerotic corpse of the old Europe fights against the force of nature determined to liberate her	Same as winner's, except for certain paranoid schizophrenics who believe they are Napoleon
Civil War	Enemies of freedom are defeated	The South shall rise again	Same as winner's, except in certain parts of Georgia, Alabama, Mississippi, Florida, Wyoming, Idaho, etc.

War	Winner's View	Loser's View	History's View
Japanese invasion of China	Horrible monsters come to kill, rape, way outstay their welcome	Glorious expansion of world's #1 civilization into territory held by stupid Chinese people	Same as winner's
World War I	Bad Germans shown who's boss	Glorious Germany shamed and victimized, but don't worry, we'll be back	Same as winner's, eventually
Vietnam	Aggression and imperialism defeated by spunky guerrilla army led by George Washington of his nation	Commie aggressors stomp out freedom-loving citizens of ancient nation	Same as winner's, except in Hollywood

Most of the time, you will note, it is the winner's account that carries the day, except in Stallone movies. This is due to the fact that the loser's side has a lot of sour grapes and what-ifs to put forth, while the winner can build on its ongoing power and success, as well as the natural, human need to believe that everything happens for a reason and that Right, in the end, will prevail.

Afterword

Can't We All Just Get Along?

You love life, and we love death.
Al Qaeda spokesman

And so, as the sun sets slowly in the west, we bid farewell to our civilization.

But not really, right? We're willing to fight for anything we believe in, and most of all we believe in perpetuating our way of life. This includes:

* Free enterprise: Translated into personal terms, it means that as a people we would like, each of us, to do pretty much what we want to do every day, and to have enough money to do it. Some of us care about whether that hurts other people, the planet, or ourselves. A lot of us don't.

* Dissent: If we want to say something, we'd like to say it. For that matter, if we want to do something, we'd like to do it. As long as it doesn't hurt anybody. That much of the late twentieth century remains. A fair number of us also wouldn't mind offering other people the same rights to speak and act freely, but not all of us.

* Media: We want iPods and twelve-disc CD changers in our minivans, and WiFi in our coffeehouses and TiVo, too. Definitely TiVo.

* Sex: Sure, we're screwed up about it, but we don't have to wait to go to heaven to get laid, even those of us who are interested in virgins.

* Smoked meats: Nobody doesn't like them, particularly sausage. Even vegetarians have this weird concoction made out of soy and some other kinds of goop that are shaped like it, to make them feel better about things.

* Consumer goods: What a vast cornucopia of great stuff we have at our fingertips, even those of us who don't have as much money as others. Just go to Costco some weekend and see people of all stations and nations mingle while acquiring vast inundations of computers and minivacs and Crest and Worcestershire sauce and Double A batteries and shrimp and greasy croissants as big as a footballs. Down the main drag there are emporia that house Home Depot and Wal-Mart and Honda and Chevy and Ford and Chrysler and sixteen kinds of vodka at the Wine Rack and supercomfortable sneakers at Foot Locker and movies targeted to our demographic at Blockbuster. If we don't know that we need something, there's an enormous machine dedicated to convincing us otherwise.

* Democracy: We'll certainly fight for our own, even if we're not sure it's our responsibility to impose it on those who would prefer to live in shackles.

* Success at work: We'll do all the reprehensible stuff we must in order to wield an amount of power appropriate to our view of ourselves and put a fresh Hostess Twinkie on our tables every night, and to feel, as we sleep in our nice toasty beds, that we have ripped the still-beating heart from the breast of our competition for yet another day.

✳ No terror: If you are reading this book, chances are you belong to that portion of the world that would prefer not to be blown up while you're on the bus on the way to work, having a party with the kids at a restaurant, or sitting in your office looking out the window.

None of these desires seem outlandish. And it's quite possible that anywhere you go on the face of this great green and blue ball of ours, the average person would be willing to sacrifice a great deal to achieve every one.

The question then arises: if most of us want to satisfy the same basic, sensible needs, why don't we all agree to join hands and live together in peace?

Imagine that! A world where everyone recognizes his or her neighbor's right to happiness, freedom of expression, cool sneakers that light up when you run, and high-def flat-screen TV sets? A world in which you and I might not agree on this or that, my brother or sister, but we also know that we share a common birthright: to achieve all that our humanity bequeaths to us in this too-short span of time we are allotted on this planet. A world, in short, of peace.

What a beautiful place that would be! Love! Tranquillity! Prosperity! We could make it a reality, my friends, if we'd but take a breath, beat our swords into plowshares, and drop our incessant fighting and squabbling for the good of each, and the good of all.

Yes, I can see us now, arm in arm, with hearts full of joy and hope, marching into a bright, safe future, a future free of hatred and bloodshed and war. Let's go out there and make it happen, fellow warriors.

And woe to anyone who stands in our way.